GREATways to Teach and Learn™

Texas History
Grades 5 - 8

Written by

Linda Chavez
and Patricia Pedigo

Edited and Produced by
Patricia Pedigo
and Dr. Roger DeSanti

©2008 Plutarch Publications, Inc. PPI -4281

ISBN 978-1-934990-00-1

GREATways to Teach and Learn: Texas History 5-8
Published by
Plutarch Publications, Inc.
U.S.A.
Email (for customer service enquires): plutarch_inc@yahoo.com
Copyright© 2008 Plutarch Publications, Inc.

Copyright © 2008, Plutarch Publications, Inc., Mandeville, Louisiana. All rights reserved. The purchase of this material entitles the buyer to reproduce worksheets and activities for classroom use only—not for commercial resale. Reproduction of these materials for an entire school or district is prohibited. No part of this book may be reproduced (except as noted above), stored in a retrieval system, or transmitted in any form or by any means (mechanically, electronically, recording, etc.) without the prior written consent of Plutarch Publications, Inc.

ISBN-13: 978-1-934990-00-1
ISBN-10: 1-934990-00-0

About the series ...

The GREATways to Teach and Learn™ series are books intended to supplement curriculum and textbooks. Sixty-four pages of activities presented in each GREATways to Teach and Learn™ book engage the learner in active practice of basic skills required at the appropriate grade level. Activities are designed with various learning styles in mind to include every child in the learning process.

Each book contains two pages of *Quick Cues,* a handy list of important vocabulary, rules, or examples of standards covered in that GREATways to Teach and Learn™ book. The page "How to Use This Book" provides suggestions and ideas for using *Quick Cues* for additional instruction or practice.

GREATways to Teach and Learn™ books are designed to comply with State Curriculum Standards. Although the level at which specific topics are mandated may vary from State to State, many State Curriculum Standards agree on the grade level at which most skills are introduced. The GREATways to Teach and Learn™ series focuses on those standards that are commonly introduced at each grade level. The Score Computation Chart (page 4) and the Standards Competency Chart (page 5) provide a viable means to assess the level at which a child is able to complete each standard presented.

The goal of this series is to provide grade appropriate standards, practice, and application in a straight-forward, easy to understand manner. Appropriate materials and presentation produce comprehension. Practice produces proficiency. Application produces students able to interact with the real world.

About the author and editors .....

Linda Chavez, **M.Ed.** in elementary education, also holds an Administrative endorsement. She has more than 25 years experience in elementary classrooms. Linda is certified and has taught in the states of Louisiana, Texas, and New Mexico.

Patricia Pedigo, **M.Ed.** in elementary education, also earned the Reading Specialist endorsement. She has more than 20 years experience in elementary and junior high classrooms and a passion for working with "learning different" children. Patricia has authored and/or edited 50 instructional books that are used in classrooms across North America.

Roger DeSanti Sr., Ed.D. in Reading and Special Education, is a Professor of Education whose area of expertise is literacy and the learning process. He has over 30 years of classroom experience working with and educating children and their teachers. Roger has over 100 publications, including 50 instructional books that are used in classrooms across North America.

Texas History Grades 5-8

The United States
Map of United States 6
Information about the U.S. 7
Map of Texas 8
State Symbols
Statistics Sheet 9
Flag and Seal 10
Bird and Flower 11
Tree and Gem 12
Find the Facts 13
Geography
Austin 14
Houston and Dallas 15
San Antonio 16
Amarillo, El Paso, Corpus Christi ... 17
City Facts 18
Population Graph 19
People 20
Regions 21
Climate 22
Temperature Table 23
Natural Resources 24
Label the Map 25
Map Facts 26
Economy 27
Quick Quiz 28
History
Early History 29

Spanish Explorers 30
American Settlers 31
The Revolution 32
Who am I? 33
Joining the U.S. 34
Civil War 35
Find the Facts 36
Frontier 37
Texas Today 38
Flags over Texas 39
History Time Line 40
Texas Time Line 41
Cause and Effect 42
Wordsearch 43
Famous Texans
Famous Texans 44
Famous Texans Crossword 45
REVIEW
Crossword Clues 46
Crossword Puzzle 47
Fact or Opinion? 48
Wordsearch 49
Unit Test 50
Unit Test 51
Unit Test 52
Unit Test 53
Extension Activities 54

State Flag of Texas

Answer Keys

Pages 13, 14, 15, 16 55
Pages 18, 19, 20, 21 56
Pages 22, 23, 25, 26 57
Pages 28, 31, 33, 34 58
Pages 36, 39, 40. 41 59
Pages 42, 43, 45, 47 60
Pages 48, 49, 50, 51 61
Pages 52, 53 62

©Plutarch Publications, Inc. PPI -4281

How to use this book ...

GREATways to Teach and Learn™ books offer several features designed to enhance the learning process and assist the teacher in assessing the learner's progress. On the next few pages you will find Quick Cues, a Score Computation Chart, a Standards Competency Chart, and recommendations based on the competency level of the learner.

QUICK CUES: This book includes two pages of *Quick Cues* which are important facts at your fingertips. The Quick Cues found on pages two and three of this book lists Texas Facts and vocabulary terms that should be studied to master the information in this book. Ways to use these pages are as varied as the number of readers, but here are a few suggestions to get started:
- √ Use the blank map on page 53 to identify all the geographical areas listed on the *Quick Cues* Texas Facts list.
- √ Ask the learner to select ten of the *Quick Cues* Vocabulary words and use them to retell a story about a related piece of Texas history.
- √ Use the *Quick Cues* sheets as a handy reference and study guide.
- √ List each word on an index card and use them as flashcards. The learner can keep the words that are correctly identified.
- √ Create a "Word Bank" box where the flashcards can be kept. Have the learner use these words to create sentences or short stories.

SCORE COMPUTATION CHART: This assessment tool can be found on page four of this book. After the learner completes an activity in this book, record the number of correct items on the score computation chart. When all pages for a listed standard have been completed, tally the number of correct answers and record it in the column on the far right (under the total of correct answers possible). Transfer the learner's totals to the chart on page five to find the level of competency.

STANDARDS COMPETENCY CHART: Use the total number correct scores from page four to identify the level at which the learner comprehends/applies the standard. The range of scores within each level (Mastery, Instructional, Basic, and Limited) are approximate indicators of how well the learner understands and can apply each standard. The degree of competency at that level will vary with the score. For example, a score of 75 in History indicates Mastery, but is close to Instructional and the learner could benefit from more practice with that standard. Recommendations based on the competency level are offered at the bottom of the page.

©Plutarch Publications, Inc. PPI -4281

Quick Cues

Texas Facts:

Major Cities
Austin - capital
Houston - largest city
Dallas
San Antonio
Amarillo
El Paso
Corpus Christi

Symbols
Flag: blue for loyalty
　　　white for purity
　　　red for bravery
State Seal:
　　oak branch for strength
　　olive branch for peace
State Bird - Mockingbird
State Flower - Bluebonnet
State Tree - Pecan
State Gem - Topaz

Rank with other States
Size: 2nd largest State
Population: 2nd largest State

Bordering States
Louisiana - east
Arkansas - northeast
Oklahoma - north
New Mexico - west
Bordering Country
Mexico - southwest
Bordering body of water
Gulf of Mexico - southeast

Rivers
Rio Grande - southwest along the Mexico border
Red River - north along the border of Oklahoma
Brazos River - southwest from the border of New Mexico to the Gulf of Mexico
Sabine River - east along the border of Louisiana
Colorado River - from the border of New Mexico extending southeast to the Gulf of Mexico
Pecos River - west from the New Mexico border to the Rio Grand on the Mexico border

Regions
Gulf Coastal Plains
North Central Plains
Great Plains
Mountains and Basins

Natural Resources
oil, salt, sulfur, gypsum, natural gas

Major Industries
petroleum and natural gas
farming - cotton and cattle
steel manufacturing
banking
insurance
tourism

©Plutarch Publications, Inc. PPI -4281

Quick Cues

Vocabulary

- Alamo
- Amarillo
- Apache
- Arkansas
- Astrodome
- Austin
- Barbara Jordan
- bluebonnet
- boundary
- bravery
- buffalo
- Caddo
- cattle ranching
- Chisholm Trail
- citrus
- Coahuiltecan
- Comanche
- Corpus Christi
- cowboy
- Dallas
- David Crockett
- de Pineda
- de Vaca
- drought
- Dwight D. Eisenhower
- El Paso
- Estevanico
- Galveston
- George Bush
- Great Depression
- Guadalupe Peak
- Gulf of Mexico
- helium
- Henry Cisneros
- Houston
- hurricane
- Johnny Rutherford
- Jumanos
- Karankawas
- La Salle
- Law of April 6, 1830
- Lee Trevino
- Louisiana
- loyalty
- Lyndon Johnson
- Mexico
- mission
- mockingbird
- New Mexico
- Nolan Ryan
- Oklahoma
- Palmito Hill
- Palo Duro Canyon
- pecan
- petroleum
- precipitation
- presidios
- purity
- Reconstruction
- Red River
- Red River Valley
- Republic of Texas
- reservation
- Rio Grande
- rural
- Sabine
- Sam Houston
- San Antonio
- Santa Anna
- secede
- Stephen Austin
- sulphur
- territory
- Texas
- the Confederacy
- the Union
- The Valley
- Tigua
- topaz
- tornado
- Tornado Alley
- urban
- William Travis
- Willie Shoemaker

©Plutarch Publications, Inc. PPI-4281

Score Computation Chart
Texas History
Grades 5 - 8

State Symbols												Score
Page number	10	11	12	13								
# possible				12								**12**
# correct												
Maps: Cities												
Page number	14	15	16	18	19	20						
# possible	7	10	10	16	7	11						**61**
# correct												
Geography												
Page number	21	22	23	25	26							
# possible	4	8	10	16	18							**56**
# correct												
History												
Page number	31	33	34	36	40	41	42					
# possible	5	12	8	16	19	8	15					**83**
# correct												
Reading Graphics												
Page number	19	20	23	39	40	41						
# possible	7	11	10	6	19	8						**61**
# correct												
Review												
Page number	28	43	45	47	48	49						
# possible	18	15	12	32	30	20						**127**
# correct												
Test												
Page number	50	51	52	53								
# possible	25	25	23	21								**94**
# correct												

©Plutarch Publications, Inc. PPI -4281

Standards Competency Chart

Step 1: After the learner completes each page, record the number correct on the Score Computation Chart (page 4). Calculate the total number correct for each standard.

Step 2: Find the learner's score for each standard in the boxes of that row. Mark the box with an X (or the learner's score) to identify the level of competency for that standard. For example, a score of 47 for the standard of Geography places the child on the "Instructional" level and a score of 52 would indicate the "Mastery" level.

Step 3: Follow the recommendation guidelines at the bottom of this page.

Standard	Mastery	Instructional	Basic	Limited
State Symbols	12 - 11	10 - 9	8 - 7	6 or below
Maps: Cities	61 - 55	54 - 46	45 - 37	36 or below
Geography	56 - 50	49 - 42	41 - 33	32 or below
History	83 - 75	74 - 62	61 - 49	48 or below
Reading Graphics	61 - 55	54 - 46	45 - 37	36 or below
Review	127 - 114	113 - 95	94 - 76	75 or below
Final Test	94 - 84	83 - 70	69 - 56	55 or below

Recommendation Guidelines

Mastery: The learner is capable of using this standard independently. Move on to the next higher grade level.

Instructional: The learner has a working understanding of the standard, but needs some guided practice on this grade level.

Basic: The learner has minimal grasp of the standard and needs direct instruction and guided practice to apply the concept fully. The learner could benefit from more instruction, review, and practice before approaching the standard at this level again.

Limited: The learner has a limited understanding of the standard and should be moved to the next lower grade level for instruction and practice.

©Plutarch Publications, Inc. PPI-4281

Name _____

Standard: Map

Map of the United States
Position of Texas

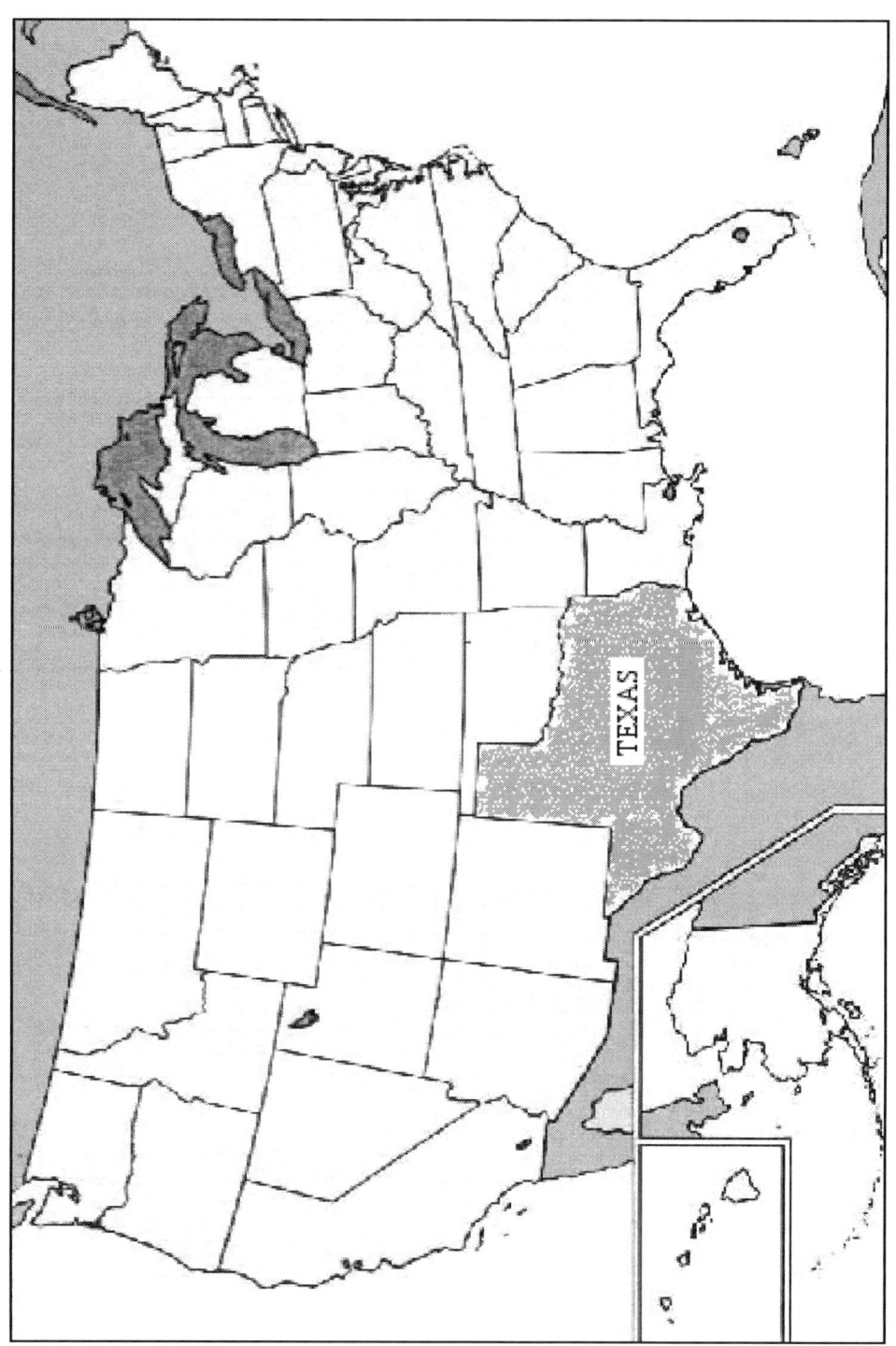

Name _____   Standard: U.S. History

The United States

In the 1400's Europeans began to explore a new continent on the other side of the Atlantic Ocean. This continent was called America. Spain, France, and England each claimed parts of America for their country. Struggles, battles, and wars broke out as these countries fought among themselves and with the native Indians for control of the land. Eventually the French settled more toward the north (the area of Canada), England claimed the middle land (generally the United States), and Spain focused on the southern end of the continent (Mexico).

By the mid 18th century the English colonists were no longer happy living under British rule. A series of events led to the American Revolution and the establishment of the United States of America. The name for this new country was chosen because each of the original thirteen colonies (now states) had their own particular problems which needed particular laws for control. The states wanted control over their needs, and yet they wanted a central government to bring all the states together under a
common set of laws.

The original thirteen states were along the eastern coast and the rest of the land to the west was fairly wild and unsettled. As people began to move west and organize into territories, they would decide on boundaries and laws to govern themselves. Eventually they would ask Congress to recognize them as a state and they would join the Union. Each new state had control over its own laws and government, but also joined the central (or Federal) government that held the country together. This process continued until all the land between the Atlantic and the Pacific, north to Canada and south to Mexico had become part of a state. There are 48 such states in this region.

The last two states admitted to the Union (Alaska and Hawaii) are the only two which are not physically near what we call the Continental United States. Alaska was a large piece of land at the northwest tip of Canada. The United States bought this land from Russia and made it the 49th state. Hawaii, a group of islands in the Pacific Ocean, became the 50th state.

Every one of these fifty states of the United States has its own symbols (flag, bird, gemstone, tree, etc.), unique geography, rich history, and famous citizens. There are wonderful tourist attractions, historical spots, natural resources, museums, cities, parks, and thousands of other interesting places in each state.

Learning more about the state you live in will help you to understand your own history and how your state helped make the United States a great country. This book will bring you information about your state. Enjoy finding out how this "wild" country was tamed and became a part of the Union!

©Plutarch Publications, Inc. PPI -4281

Name _____   Standard: Reading Maps

Map of Texas
Major Cities, Rivers, Regions, and Bordering States

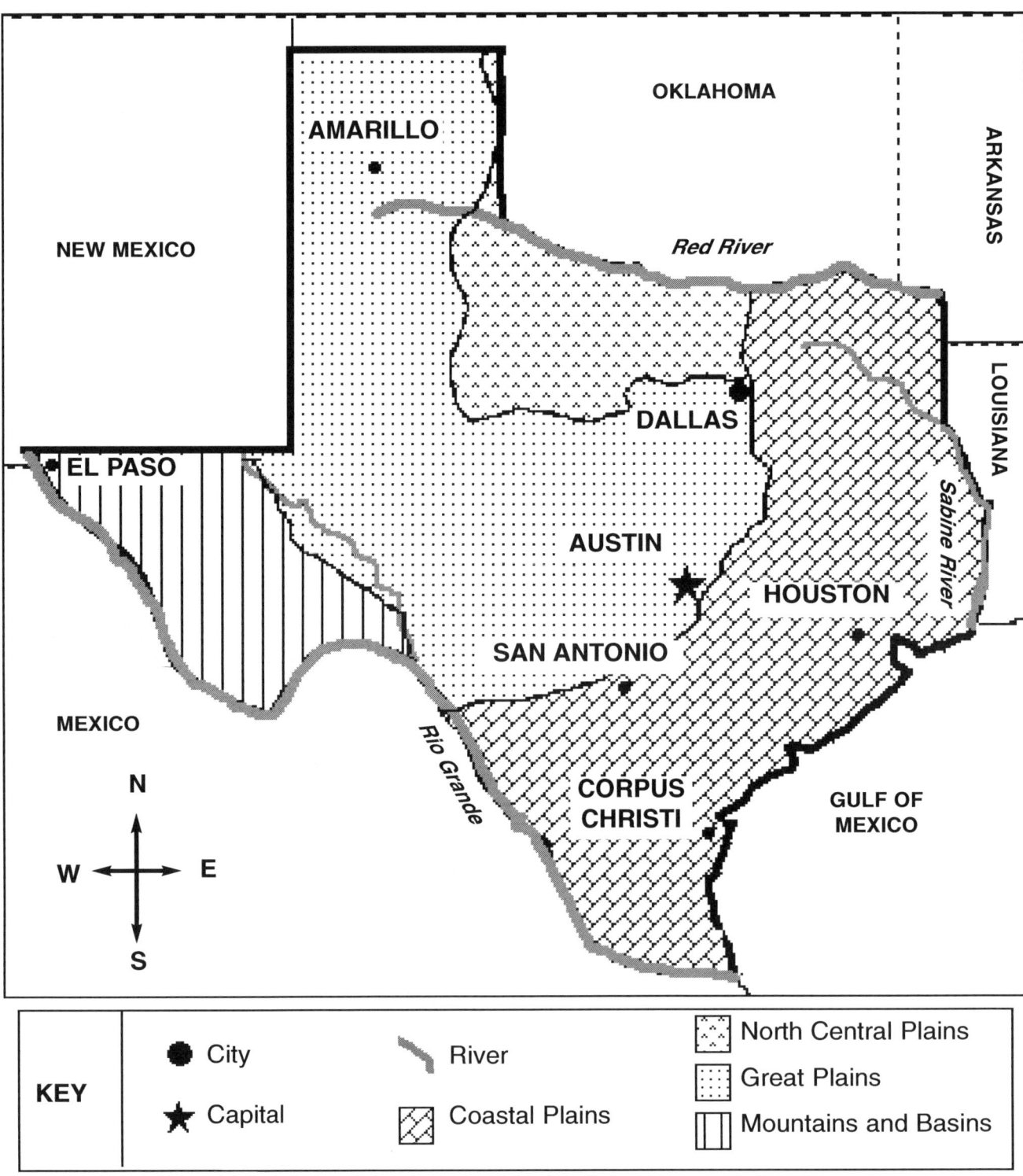

Name _____   Standard: State Facts

Texas Fact Chart

Statehood: December 29, 1845
State number: 28th
Capital City: Austin
Largest City: Houston
Size Rank: 2nd largest state
Area in square miles: 268,601
Greatest Distance North to South: 801 miles
Greatest Distance East to West: 774 miles
Population (2006 Census): 23,507,793
Population Rank: 2nd largest state
Population Distribution: 80% urban
                          20% rural
Counties: 254
Colleges and Universities: 184
Government: 2 senators
             32 representatives
Elevation: highest point - 8,749 feet at Guadalupe Peak
             lowest point - 0 feet at the Gulf of Mexico
State Flower: bluebonnet
State Bird: mockingbird
State Tree: pecan
Nickname: Lone Star State
Named for: Spanish "tejas" and Indian "techas" meaning "friends"
State Song: Texas, Our Texas
Borders: Louisiana is on the east; Arkansas on the northeast; Oklahoma on the north; New Mexico on the northwest; Mexico on the southwest; and the Gulf of Mexico on the southeast.

Name _____   Standard: State Symbols

Symbols are pictures or colors that represent ideas or feelings. Each state has a flag, seal, bird, flower, tree, and gem that represents an idea or tells us something about that state.

State Flag

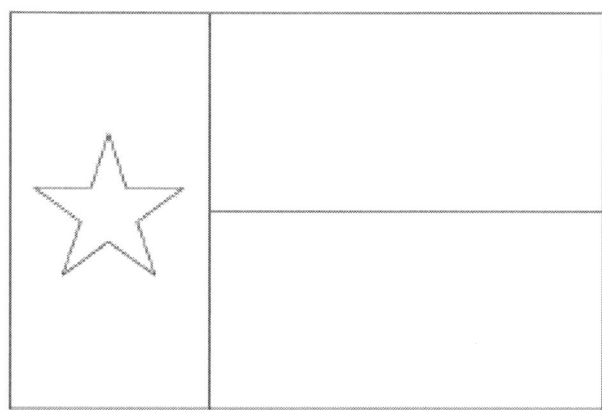

Color the flag
Star - white
Panel behind star - blue
Panel at top right - white
Panel on bottom right - red

The flag of Texas is simple in design. The flag is divided into three sections and the colors are red, white, and blue (the same colors found in the flag of the United States). A panel of blue parallels the flag pole and contains one white star at the center. The color blue is said to stand for loyalty. The single star is the reason Texas has the nickname "The Lone Star State". The rest of the flag is divided in half horizontally (from left to right) into two panels. The top panel is white, representing purity. The bottom panel is red and stands for bravery.

State Seal

The state seal of Texas is seen on government offices and used on official state papers. The present seal was adopted in 1846 and features a circle with a single white star of five points on a blue background. Two tree branches are united and encircle the star. The branch on the left is from an oak tree and symbolizes strength. The branch to the right consists of olive leaves and represents peace. An outside border contains the words "The State of Texas".

©Plutarch Publications, Inc. PPI-4281

Name ——————————————————————— Standard: State Symbols

Symbols are pictures or colors that represent ideas or feelings. Each state has a flag, seal, bird, flower, tree, and gem that represents an idea or tells us something about that state.

State Bird

In 1927 the mockingbird became the state bird of Texas. This bird is known for its exceptional ability to imitate familiar sounds. One type of mockingbird was recorded mimicking the songs of 36 other species. It has been noted that mockingbirds can even imitate the sound of farm tractors! Unlike most birds, both the male and female birds have the same coloring of gray with a grayish-white breast. These birds grow about 9 to 11 inches in length. Most mockingbirds that live in the south build their nests in low trees and bushes. Mockingbirds help man by eating harmful insects and a variety of weed seeds.

State Flower

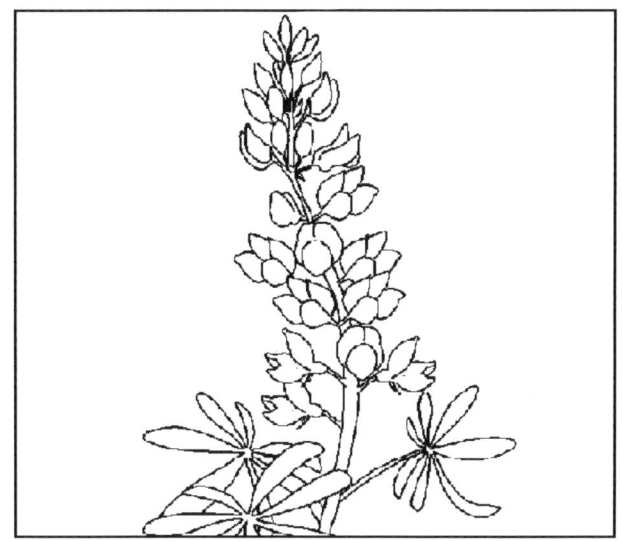

The state flower of Texas is the bluebonnet which is native to many areas of the state. In late March and early April masses of these beautiful blue flowers cover roadsides and meadows. The tiny blossoms of the flower are shaped like a woman's bonnet and grow one above the other along the stem. The flowers have a white center.

©Plutarch Publications, Inc. PPI -4281

Name _____

Standard: State Symbols

Symbols are pictures or colors that represent ideas or feelings. Each state has a flag, seal, bird, flower, tree, and gem that represents an idea or tells us something about that state.

State Tree

The state tree of Texas is the pecan. These trees grow abundantly in the forests of Texas and along the banks of rivers and streams. Some trees can produce up to 500 pounds of nuts each year. The nuts are gathered after they have fallen from the tree. Besides producing the valuable fruit, the wood is used to make furniture, flooring, and various other wood products. A former Texas governor liked the trees so much that he had them distributed so they could be planted throughout the state. He also ordered that a pecan tree be planted by his grave.

State Gem

Topaz, the birthstone of November, has been chosen as the state gem of Texas. It is a highly valued gemstone that forms into large transparent crystals. Topaz varies in color and may be formed in hues of pale blue, shades of brown, straw yellow, and some may even be colorless. This gem is found in high-temperature veins or in granite, where it is the last mineral to form. It is collected in several areas of central Texas.

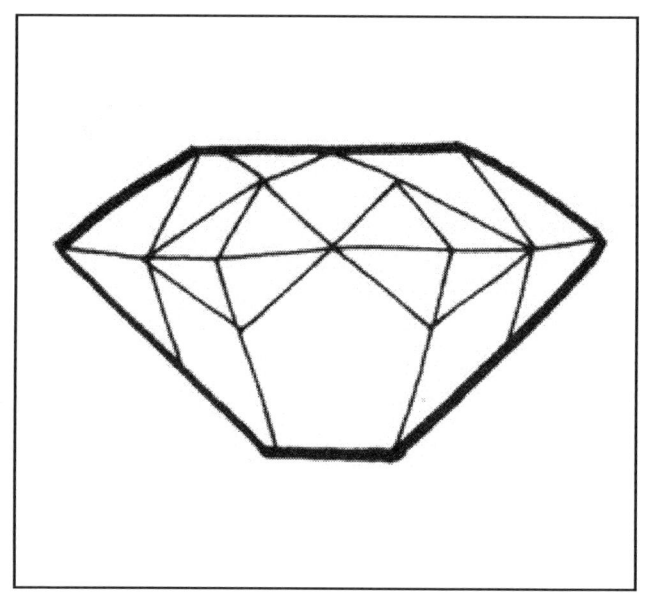

©Plutarch Publications, Inc. PPI-4281

Name _____   Standard: State Symbols

Find the Facts

1. What does the word "symbol" mean? _____
   _____

2. What do the three colors on the Texas state flag represent?

   blue _____   white _____   red _____

3. Why was Texas nicknamed the "Lone Star State"? _____
   _____

4. Where will you always see the State Seal? _____
   _____

5. What do the olive and oak branches symbolize on the State Seal? ____
   _____

6. What words are found on the Texas State Seal? _____
   _____

7. In what year did the mockingbird become the State Bird of Texas? ____
   _____

8. What makes the mockingbird so unusual? _____
   _____

9. Why do you think the bluebonnet was chosen as the State Flower? ____
   _____

10. What is the State Tree of Texas? _____
    _____

11. What products are made from the State Tree? _____
    _____

12. What is the Texas State Gem? _____

Name _____

Standard: Major Cities

Austin: The Capital

In 1839 the village of Waterloo, built on the Colorado River in central Texas, was selected as the state capital. It was renamed Austin for Stephen F. Austin, sometimes called the Father of Texas. In 1842 Austin was under frequent raids from Mexicans and Indians, so the government offices were moved to Houston until they could return to Austin in 1845.

Austin is noted as an education center with the huge campus of University of Texas located there. It is also known as the "Live Music Capital of the World" with many live music clubs on famous Sixth Street. Austin is a beautiful city with broad, tree lined streets and hills rising from the river. It grew rapidly during the 1980's and has become a popular tourist city. A 2005 Census shows the metropolitan population to be 690,252 which makes it the 16th largest city in the United States. The climate for this area is mild with an average temperature of 68° and a yearly rainfall of 31 inches.

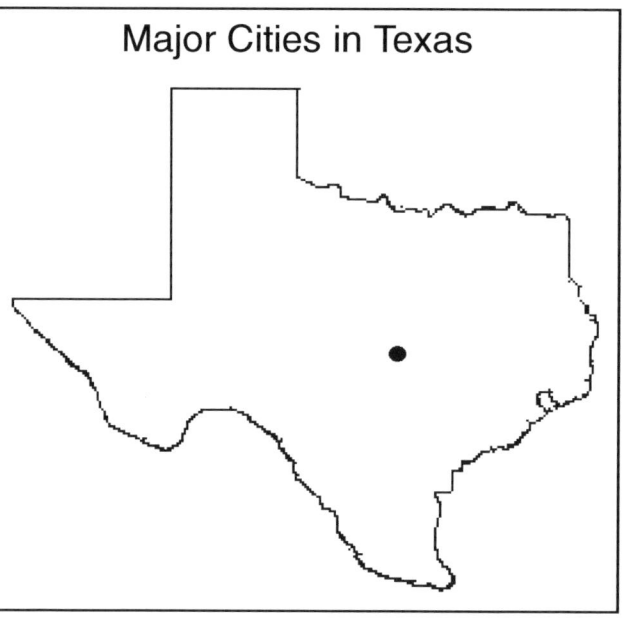

Major Cities in Texas

The state capital building, completed in 1888, sits on one of the hills rising up from the river. Land in western Texas was sold to pay for the new building. The nation's capital in Washington, D.C. was used as a model for the Texas capital building. It is made of pink granite that was taken from Marble Falls, Texas. The building covers three acres of land and has over eighteen acres of floor space.

1. Label Austin on the map.
   List three facts about the city of Austin.
2. _____
3. _____
4. _____
5. Of what stone is the Austin capital building made? _____
6. What was the original name of Austin? _____
7. Why were the state offices moved to Houston in 1842? _____

©Plutarch Publications, Inc. PPI -4281

Name _____

Standard: Major Cities

Houston and Dallas

Houston, the largest city in Texas and the third largest in the country, is located in southeast Texas. It was founded in 1836 and named for Sam Houston, a famous Texan. Houston was the capital of the Republic of Texas until was moved to Austin in 1845.

Houston, with a population of 2,009,690 (2003 Census), is a leading center for refining oil and producing chemicals. Although it is 80 km (50 mi.) from the Gulf of Mexico, a connecting waterway makes Houston the third busiest port in the country. Southeast of Houston is the Johnson Space Center. Astronauts are trained and mission control for all space flights are directed from here. Houston is also home of the Astrodome, the first domed stadium built in the United States.

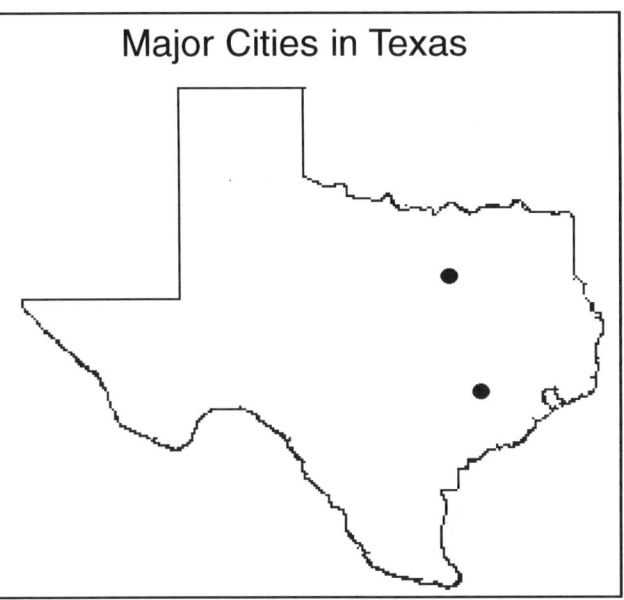

Dallas, with a population of 1,208,318 (2005 Census), is the second largest city in the state. It is located on Trinity River prairie flats of northeastern Texas. It was founded in 1841 and was named for George Dallas, the Vice President of the United States at that time. During its early years Dallas was a cotton marketing center. Today that past is still remembered with the New Year's Day football game known as the "Cotton Bowl". Dallas has become a center for banking, insurance companies, and fashion design. It is the home of the professional football team the Dallas Cowboys and has one of the largest year round farmer's market in the nation. Ft. Worth, just to the west of Dallas, is so close the cities are called the Dallas/Ft. Worth area. Their combined population is about 4,000,000.

1. Label Houston and Dallas on the map.
2. Compare these two cities by filling in the chart below:

	Population	Founded	Named for	Location	Point of interest
Houston					
Dallas					

©Plutarch Publications, Inc. PPI-4281

Name _____   Standard: Major Cities

San Antonio

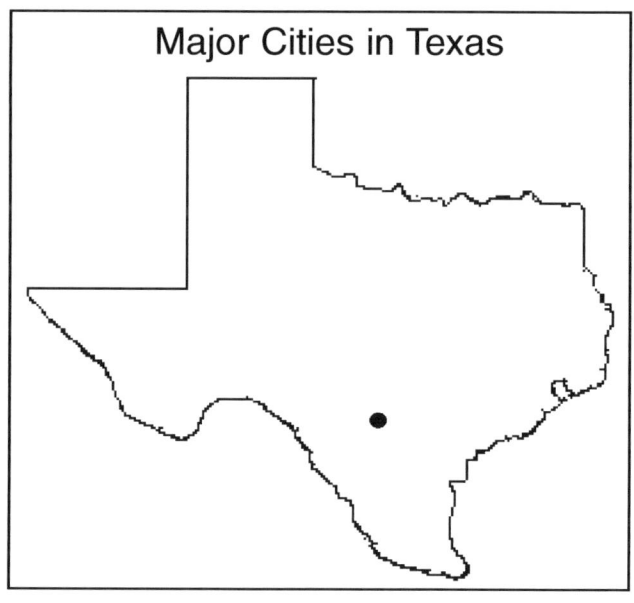

Major Cities in Texas

San Antonio, with a population of 1,256,509 (2005 Census) is the third largest city in Texas, and the 7th largest in the United States. It was founded in 1796 as a Spanish garrison (fort) with several small missions nearby. Early Spanish and Mexican pioneer families came to these missions to live and work. One mission, the Alamo, became an important battle site when Texas fought for its independence from Mexico in 1836. San Antonio was also located at the beginning of the Chisholm Trail, a famous trail for driving cattle from Texas to Kansas where they would be sold and shipped further east. Because of its rich history and Mexican/Spanish roots, the city has a very distinctive style of architecture and a unique culture which has made it a huge tourist attraction.

1. Label San Antonio on the map.
   List three facts about the city of San Antonio:
2. _____
3. _____
4. _____
5. In what year was San Antonio founded? _____
   What two nationalities originally settled in San Antonio?
   6. _____   7. _____
8. Which mission in San Antonio became famous in 1836?
   _____

   What two things found in San Antonio are unusual because of the blending of the Spanish and Mexican peoples?
   9. _____   10. _____

©Plutarch Publications, Inc. PPI-4281

Name _____   Standard: Major Cities

**Amarillo
El Paso
Corpus Christi**

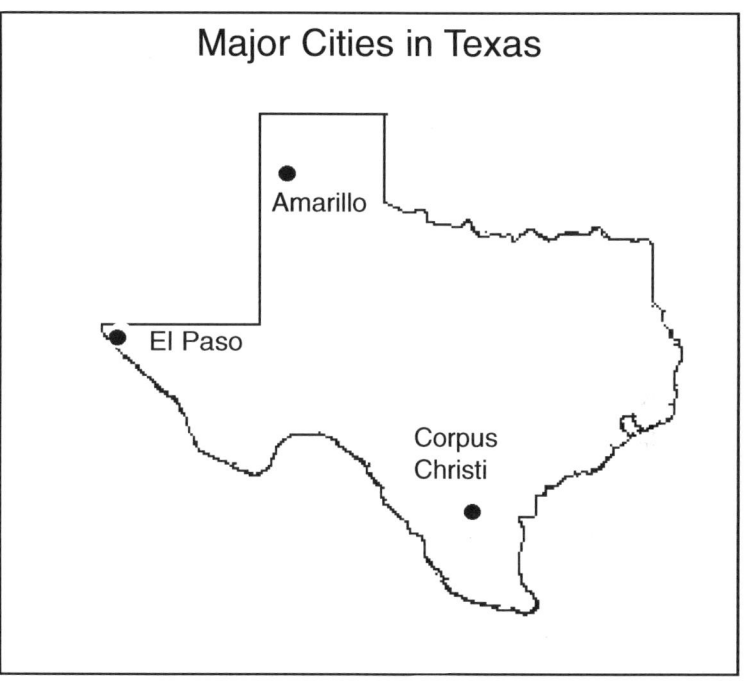

Amarillo is the largest city in the texas panhandle. It was founded in 1887 when it became the spot where two railroads crossed. The name Amarillo is Spanish for "yellow", the color of the clay found in the soil there. The city continued to grow when oil and gas were discovered there in the early 1900's. Today the city's population is about 178,612 (2005 Census). Amarillo is known as a major producer of helium as well as a meat packing center for the herds of cattle raised in the area. The many grain elevators and the huge cattle auctions give the city a definite western flavor. The beautiful Palo Duro Canyon State Park is located just outside of the city.

El Paso, located in the far west corner of the state, is on the Rio Grande river just across from Juarez, Mexico. It was named in 1598 by Juan de Onate, a colonizer of New Mexico. El Paso is Spanish for "the pass", and was named this because it was part of a well traveled route for settlers headed north. The first Spanish settlements in Texas appeared in this city. With a population of about 598,590 (2005 Census), El Paso is the commercial and industrial center of this mining and cattle raising area. Farms in the area raise fruit, cotton, and vegetables.

The popular resort community of Corpus Christi is located on Corpus Christi Bay. It was named by Alonso de Pineda in 1519 for the bay on which it sits. Corpus Christi Bay is separated from the Gulf of Mexico by Mustang Island (a state park) and Padre Island. The area has a warm climate and beautiful beaches, making it a tourist attraction year round. Cement, chemicals, and fishing are the leading industries in the area. Corpus Christi is also a busy port that exports goods such as cotton, petroleum, and sulfur. It has a population of about 279,208 (2005 Census).

©Plutarch Publications, Inc. PPI -4281

Name _____   Standard: Major Cities

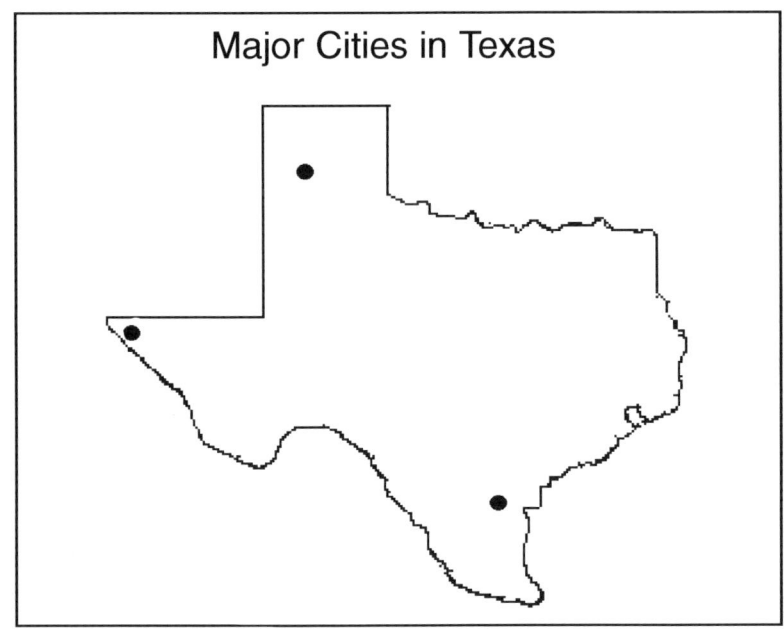

**Amarillo
El Paso
Corpus Christi
Fact Sheet**

1. Label Amarillo, El Paso, and Corpus Christi on the map.
List these three cities and their population in order from largest to smallest.

2. _____
3. _____
4. _____

Write the name of the city after the facts that describe it.

5. I am a major port in the southeast of Texas. _____
6. Palo Duro State Park is just outside my city limits. _____
7. I got my name from the clay found here. _____
8. My beaches and warm climate attract tourists. _____
9. I am just across the river from Mexico. _____
10. I was named for a bay. _____
11. Fruits, cotton, and vegetables are raised on my farms. _____
12. I am the world leader in production of helium. _____
13. The first Spanish settlements in Texas were here. _____
14. I have a state park named Mustang Island. _____
15. I am found on the Rio Grande River. _____
16. I am the largest city in the Texas panhandle. _____

©Plutarch Publications, Inc. PPI-4281

Name _____   Standard: Major Cities Graphics

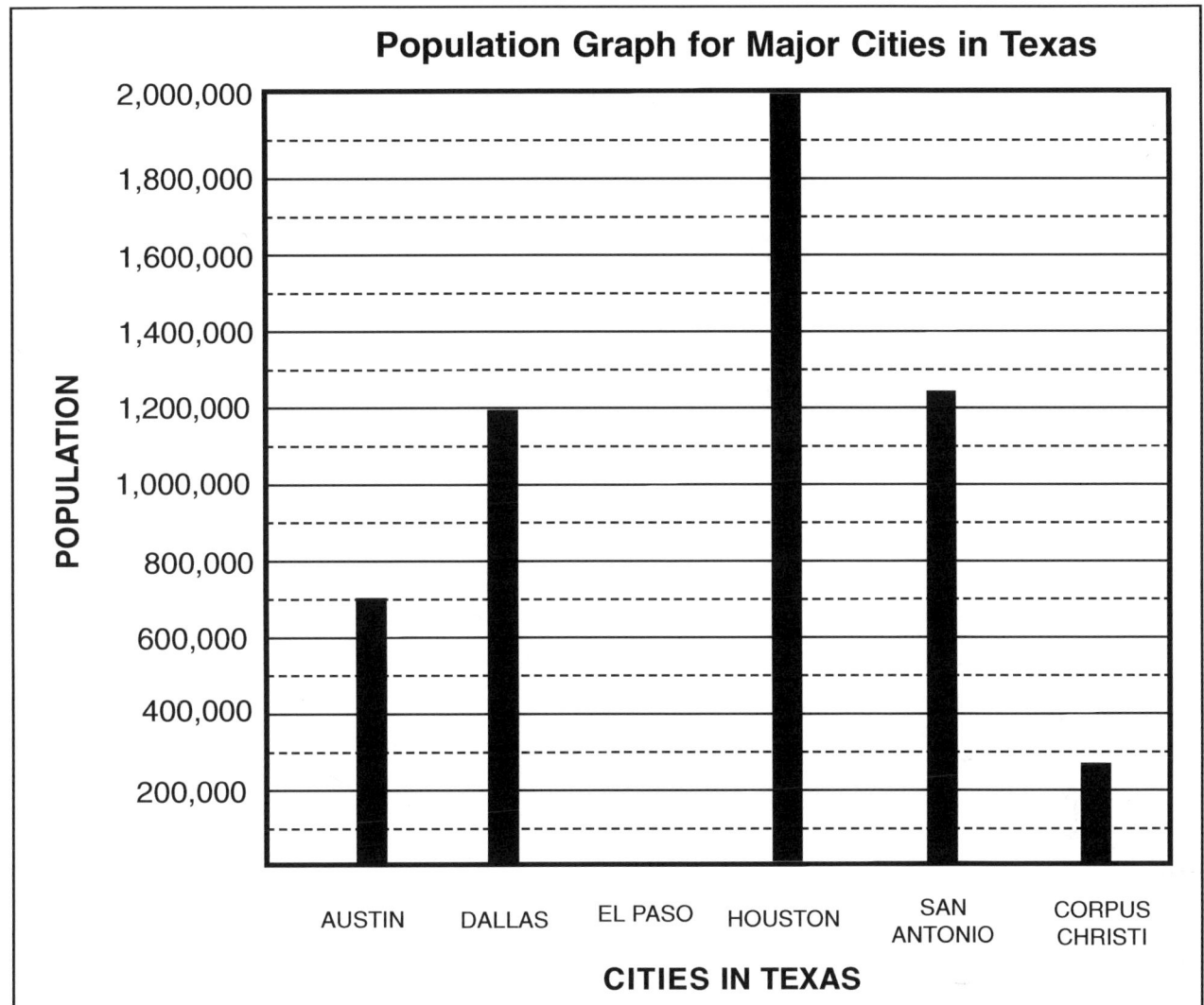

1. Add a bar to the graph to show that El Paso has a population of 600,000.
2. What is the population of Dallas and San Antonio together? _____
3. Which cities have a larger population than Austin? _____
_____
4. How much smaller is the population of Corpus Christi than Austin?
_____
5. Which pair has a higher population?
       El Paso and Austin   Dallas and Corpus Christi
6. By how much is Houston larger than Dallas? _____
7. What is the population of the two smallest cities added together?
_____

©Plutarch Publications, Inc. PPI -4281

Name _____   Standard: Major Cities Graphics

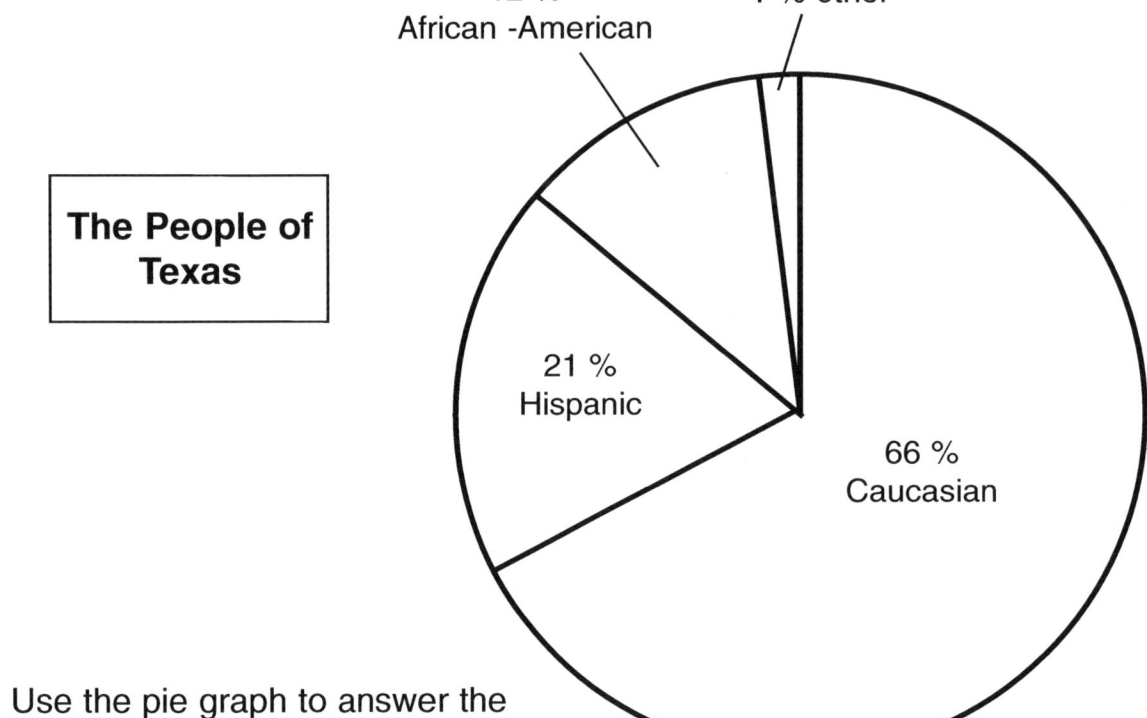

The People of Texas

Use the pie graph to answer the following questions:

1. Which group of people make up sixty-six percent of the Texas population?
   _____
2. Are there more Hispanic or African Americans living in Texas? _____
3. Which group makes up one percent of the population? _____
4. What is the difference in percentage between Caucasians and Hispanics?
   _____
5. Twenty-one percent means how many out of every one hundred? _____
6. How much of the population is made up of Hispanic and African-American?
   _____

List the nationalities in order from smallest to largest.

7. _____
8. _____
9. _____
10. _____
11. Which two nationalities make up 78 % of the total population?
    _____

©Plutarch Publications, Inc. PPI -4281

Name _____

Standard: Geography

Regions of Texas

Texas can be divided into four natural regions: the Coastal Plains in the east and southeast; the North Central Plains from the north to the center of the state; the Great Plains extending from north to south central; and the Mountains and Basins in the far southwest.

Close to one third of Texas is in the Coastal Plains region. This is the area that follows along the coast of the Gulf of Mexico and goes inland about 80 to 100 kilometers (50-60 miles). The Coastal Plains stretch across the rolling hilly lands of eastern Texas, including the forested lands in the northeast. The highest elevation (distance above sea level) is 150 meters (500 ft.). The western side of this region is a fertile belt of land called the Blackland Prairie. Houston, Dallas, Austin, San Antonio, and Corpus Christi are the largest cities in this region.

The North Central Plains region is mainly covered with farms and ranches. This region begins at the Oklahoma border and reaches south to about the middle of Texas. The land here is a little higher and more hilly than that of the Coastal Plains. Fort Worth, Arlington, and Abilene are the major cities in this region.

The Great Plains region covers a long strip extending from the northern tip of Texas to the border of Mexico. The lands in the Great Plains region are flat tablelands with an elevation of up to 1,200 meters (4,000 ft.). The region includes many areas with rich farm land. Major cities are Amarillo, Lubbock, Midland, and Odessa.

The region in the far southeastern corner of Texas is called the Mountains and Basins. The highest elevations in Texas are found here in the Guadalupe and Davis Mountains with the highest point at 2,667 meters (8,749 ft.). Rolling hills run along the Pecos River Valley. El Paso is the largest city in this region.

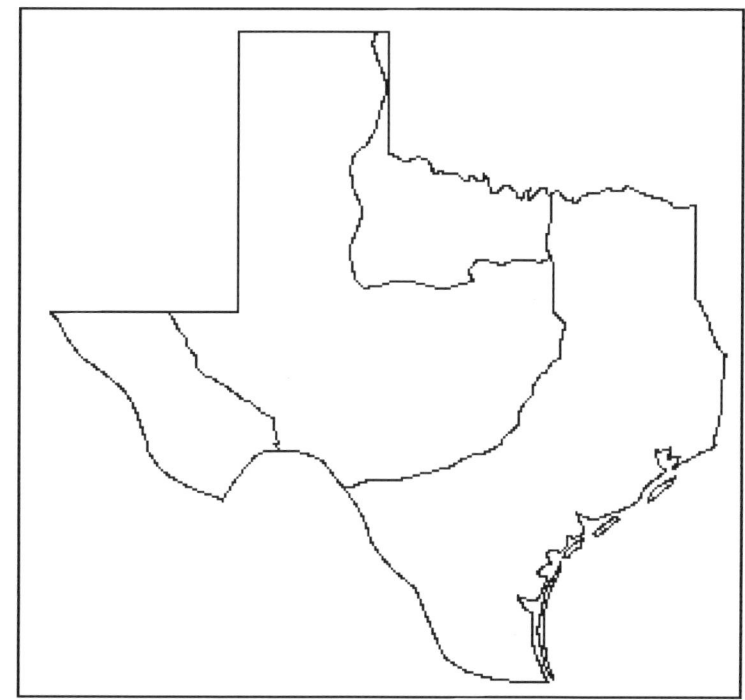

Use the information above to label the four regions of Texas on this map.

©Plutarch Publications, Inc. PPI -4281

Name _____   Standard: Geography

Climate

Texas has a broad range in climate. In southern Texas, summer temperatures can rise as high as 49° C (120°F) and do not usually go much lower than 20°C (50° F) in the winter months. However, winter temperatures in the west and northern parts of Texas can be much colder. For example, Amarillo (in the northern panhandle) gets snow every year and often has temperatures below freezing. Some areas may get as cold as -31° C (23° F) during the winter.

Precipitation, the amount of moisture that falls to earth, varies greatly across the state. An area in extreme west Texas receives an average of less than eight inches a year while parts of eastern Texas along the Sabine River average more than 59 inches per year.

Texas also has its share of floods, droughts, tornadoes, and hurricanes. Floods occur in many areas that are generally very dry. If large amounts of rain fall in a short period, the hardened ground cannot absorb the water fast enough and it quickly builds up to high levels. Droughts are long periods of dry weather with little or no precipitation. During droughts grasses die, causing the topsoil to turn to dust and blow away.

Texas is no stranger to the dangerous and sometimes deadly storm called the tornado. An average of one hundred tornadoes are sighted in Texas each year. The Red River Valley, an area that crosses northern Texas, has earned the nickname "Tornado Alley" because it is the frequent target of these storms. No other state is hit by as many tornadoes as Texas.

Hurricanes occur when tropical storms form over the warm waters of the Gulf of Mexico. As these tropical storms grow in size they may become hurricanes which sometimes hit the Texas coast. When these huge storms come ashore they can push water from the Gulf several miles inland. They begin to die as they continue over the land, dumping large amounts of rain over the area as they go. One of the most destructive hurricanes ever hit Galveston in 1900, killing over 6,000 people. Over the years forecasters have become very good at predicting where a hurricane will land, allowing people more time to move to safer areas.

What are the warmest and coolest temperatures of the Texas climate?
1. warmest _____   2. coolest _____
3. In what year was Galveston hit by a deadly hurricane? _____
What is the average annual rainfall in eastern and western Texas?
4. eastern _____   5. western _____
6. What is a drought? _____
7. What is the average number of tornadoes spotted in Texas per year? _____
8. Which state reports more tornadoes than Texas? _____

©Plutarch Publications, Inc. PPI -4281

Name _____   Standard: Geography Graphics

Average Fahrenheit Temperatures in Texas - Maximum/Minimum

	JAN.	FEB.	MAR.	APR.	MAY	JUNE	JULY	AUG.	SEPT.	OCT.	NOV.	DEC.
Amarillo	49/24	53/27	60/36	70/42	78/52	89/62	92/66	91/65	83/57	73/46	59/32	51/26
Austin	60/41	64/44	71/49	78/57	85/65	92/72	95/74	96/74	90/69	82/60	70/48	63/43
Corpus Christi	67/47	70/51	74/56	80/63	85/69	91/74	94/75	94/75	90/71	85/65	74/54	69/50
Dallas	56/36	60/39	67/45	75/55	83/63	91/72	95/75	95/75	88/67	79/57	66/44	58/38
El Paso	56/32	62/37	68/41	77/50	86/58	94/67	94/69	92/68	88/62	79/52	66/38	58/33
Houston	62/46	66/50	71/54	78/61	85/67	90/74	92/75	93/75	89/71	82/63	71/53	64/47
San Antonio	62/42	66/45	72/50	79/58	85/65	92/72	94/74	94/73	89/69	82/60	70/49	65/42

Use this table to answer the questions below.

1. Which city has the highest average temperature during the month of August? _____

2. Give the difference in the low average between Amarillo and Houston in July: _____

3. El Paso's lowest high temperature is during what month? _____

4. What are the two hottest months for Dallas? _____

5. What two cities have the same average high in February? _____

6. How many months do Dallas and El Paso have the same average high temperature? _____

7. What is the difference between the average high and low in El Paso during June? _____

8. What city has three months when the average low is below freezing? _____

9. In what month do Austin and Dallas have the same average low temperature? _____

10. What is the warmest month for Austin? _____

©Plutarch Publications, Inc. PPI-4281

Name _____

Standard: Geography

Natural Resources

A natural resource is something provided by nature that is very useful to people. Water, land, forests, and minerals are examples of natural resources. We use natural resources to grow the food we eat and to help produce the goods we use. Texas is a state very rich in natural resources.

Water is one natural resource that we cannot live without. Growing crops and raising animals would be impossible without water. Texas is second only to Alaska in its volume of inland water. There are more than 5,175 square miles of lakes, rivers, streams, and reservoirs in Texas. Reservoirs are places where water is collected and stored for use. For example, the western part of Texas gets little rainfall, not enough to grow crops or raise animals. Reservoirs are used to irrigate the land so crops can grow.

Most of the rivers in Texas flow southeast and empty into the Gulf of Mexico. Some of the boundaries, or borders, of Texas are formed by rivers. The Rio Grande is the longest river in the state and it forms the southern boundary between Texas and the country of Mexico. Part of the northern boundary between Texas and Oklahoma is from by the Red River. On the eastern boundary, the Sabine River separates Texas from the state of Louisiana. The Colorado and Brazos are long rivers that cut across Texas from the border of New Mexico to the Gulf of Mexico.

Another important resource in Texas is the land. Almost 80 percent of the land area is used for farming or ranching, nearly twice as much as any other state. The northern prairies (flat grasslands with few trees) is used for raising cattle, sheep, and goats. It is also used for growing crops such as cotton, wheat, peanuts, and sorghum. Texas produces more cattle, sheep, and sorghum than any other state. The fertile lands along the Rio Grande River in southernmost Texas is an area known as "The Valley". A warm climate and large amounts of rainfall make this area excellent for growing citrus fruits (oranges, lemons, grapefruit, etc.)

Close to one seventh of the land in Texas is covered with forest. The "Piney Woods" is an important area located in eastern Texas along the Sabine River. The pine harvested here produces lumber and plywood used to make furniture, houses, and other wood products. The pulp (sawdust and small bits of wood) is mixed with chemicals to produce paper. The state of Texas has four national forests and two national grasslands.

Since 1928 Texas has been the largest producer of petroleum in the United States. Petroleum, or crude oil, is the substance from which gasoline and diesel fuel are made. This natural resource, taken from the ground, is the most important mineral found in Texas. This state also produces large amounts of sulphur, a bright yellow mineral used in medicines, shampoo, and storage batteries. Other minerals found in Texas include natural gas, coal, gypsum, helium, talc, and salt.

©Plutarch Publications, Inc. PPI -4281

Name _____   Standard: Geography

Map of Important Cities and Areas in Texas

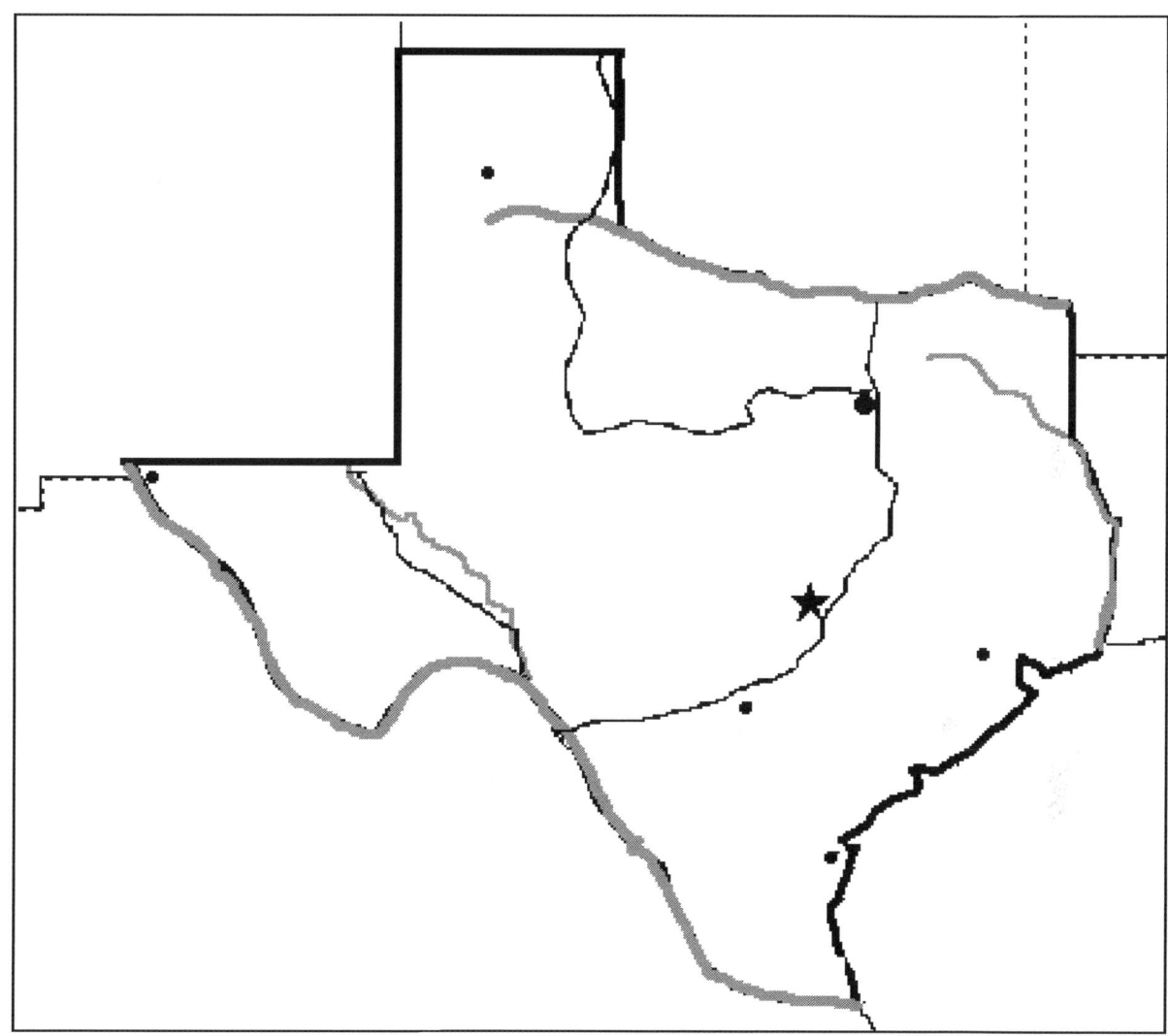

Label these places on the map:

Amarillo	Dallas	Houston	Rio Grande
Austin	El Paso	Mexico	Sabine River
Corpus Christi	Gulf of Mexico	Red River	San Antonio

Color each region:

Coastal Plains: Green
Great Plains: Blue
North Central Plains: Orange
Mountains and Basins: Brown

Name _____   Standard: Geography

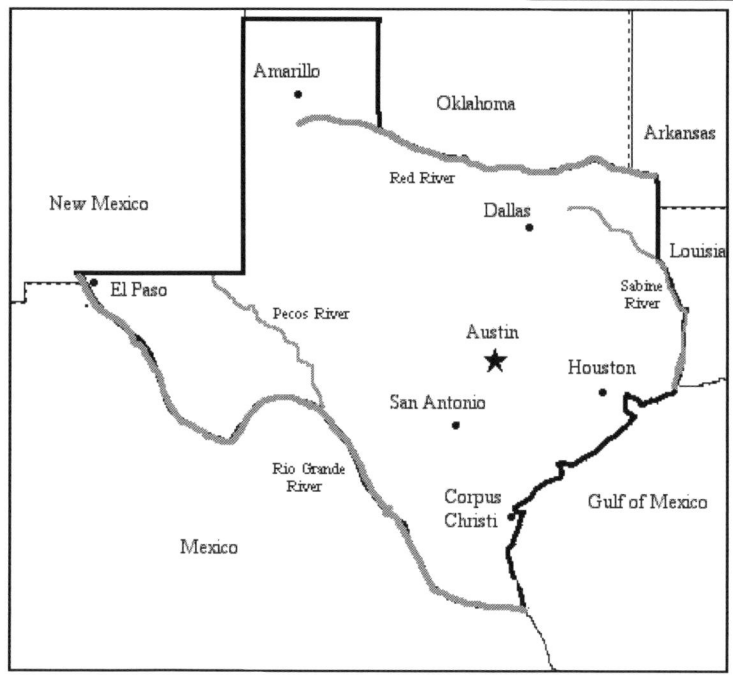

USE THE MAP AND TEXAS FACT SHEET TO ANSWER THESE QUESTIONS:
1. Texas has a total of _____ square miles.
2. Texas is the _____ largest state.
3. The state of _____ borders most of northern Texas.
4. The state of _____ borders Texas on the west.
5. Texas and _____ border on the Sabine River.
6. _____ borders on the north and east corner of Texas.
7. The country of _____ lies to the south of Texas.
8. _____ is a major body of water to the southeast of Texas.
9. Texas and Mexico are separated by _____ .
10. Austin is _____ of Dallas. (Which direction?)
11. Houston is _____ of San Antonio. (Which direction?)
12. El Paso is _____ of Dallas/Ft. Worth. (Which direction?)

True or False
13. Houston is in the southwest corner of Texas.   T   F
14. The Red River separates Texas and Louisiana.   T   F
15. The capital of Texas is Austin.   T   F
16. Texas is the largest of the fifty states.   T   F
17. Amarillo is in the panhandle.   T   F
18. Fruit is grown in "The Valley" in south Texas .   T   F

©Plutarch Publications, Inc. PPI-4281

Name _____   Standard: Geography

Economy

  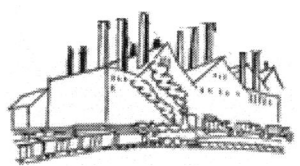 

During the 1920's huge deposits of oil were discovered in Texas. Oil was necessary to fuel machinery and many countries needed this valuable resource. Texas economy relied on the oil industry because it produced much of the state's wealth. However, in the late 1980's the world market for oil fell sharply. Other countries were producing more oil than the world needed at that time. The price of oil dropped rapidly and the oil companies in Texas began to suffer loses in profit. Many people lost their jobs during that time because it was not necessary to drill for more oil. The "black gold" of Texas no longer produced as much money for the state.

This experience moved Texans to look for other sources of income. They decided not to rely so heavily on oil, but to find new services and industries that could keep the state as wealthy as it had been. The state began to focus more on the areas of manufacturing, mining, farming, fishing, and tourism. Texas now leads the country in the manufacturing of chemicals, plastics, helium, and refined oil. It is also a large producer of paints and airplanes. Mining industries have grown as well. Texas supplies one third of the natural gas for the United States and about one fourth of its oil. This state also produces magnesium, sulfur, sand and gravel, stone, talc, sodium, and iron.

There are about 185,000 farms and ranches in Texas, more than any other state. These farms produce cotton, watermelons, rice, peanuts, pecans, hay, grapefruit, and oranges. Texas often ranks third in the nation for gross farm income (amount of money produced by farm products). Texan ranches produce more cattle, horses, and sheep than any other state. There are usually over 13 million head of cattle produced in Texas every year.

With the Gulf of Mexico right off the coast, it is easy to understand why the fishing industry is a boost to the economy. Texas leads the country in shrimping and produces large amounts of oysters, crabs, red snapper, and flounder.

Texas attracts millions of out-of-state visitors annually. Popular cities to visit include Dallas, San Antonio, Houston, El Paso, and Austin. Places of special interest are Nacogdoches (one of the oldest cities in the state) and the Lyndon B. Johnson space Center near Houston. Many tourists visit Big Bend or Guadalupe Mountains (two national parks) or one of the many recreational areas in the state. Other popular attractions are natural sports such as hunting and fishing as well as professional and college level sporting events.

©Plutarch Publications, Inc. PPI -4281

Name _____   Standard: Review

Quick Quiz

1. The city of Austin was named after what person?

2. In 1842, the capital of Texas was moved from Austin to what other city?

3. What stone is the Texas State Capital Building made of and from where was the stone taken?

4. For what famous person was the city of Houston named?

5. What famous sports arena is located in Houston?

6. The city of Dallas was named after what person?

7. What football game is held in Dallas on New Year's Day?

8. Near what city is the Alamo located?

9. What city is close to Palo Duro Canyon in the panhandle?

10. What city takes its name from the Spanish term for "the pass"?

11. What popular resort city has Mustang Island in its bay?

12. Where is "Tornado Alley"?

13. What kind of storm forms over the Gulf of Mexico, often hitting the Texas coast?

14. What is the richest natural resource in Texas?

15. Name three rivers that form boundaries for the state of Texas.

16. What are the two major uses of land in Texas?

17. What is the name of a large wooded area in eastern Texas?

18. Texas produces more of which fishing product than any other state.

©Plutarch Publications, Inc. PPI-4281

Name _____ Standard: History

Early History

About 12,000 years ago the first people arrived in Texas. Those ancient Indians came from Asia and hunted wild animals such as mammoths and mastodons. Besides hunting, they also found food in the form of berries, nuts, and the roots of some plants. These early people were nomadic Indians, moving from place to place in search of better hunting as the herds of animals moved away. Several Indian tribes lived in Texas by the year 1500 A.D.

The Karankawas were one early tribe of Indians who lived along the coast of the Gulf of Mexico. The name Karankawa means "dog lovers" and the tribe was named for the many dogs they kept with them. These indians lived a simple life that changed little over a span of hundreds of years. They hunted small game and fished from dugout canoes made of hollowed logs. The Karankawa tribe sometimes ate their enemies, believing that doing so would give them the power and courage of that person.

The Coahuiltecan Indians lived farther south along the Gulf Coast. They had few tools, were nomads like the Karankawas, and were known for their strength. The Jumanos lived in West Texas. They were mostly farmers who grew corn and hunted buffalo. They sometimes traded with Indians from east Texas.

The Caddo Indians were a smaller Indian tribe who lived in east Texas. They reached a more advanced stage of civilization than any other tribe in Texas. The Caddo worked together, mainly farming and fishing in the rivers. They were very modern in their leadership, choosing women for their chiefs as early as the 1500's. They called each other "tayshas" which means "friends". Years later the Spaniards changed the word to "texas".

Two tribes of Indians that migrated to Texas from other areas of the United States were the Comanche and Apache. These people lived off the buffalo herds, using the animals to make clothing, houses, ropes, saddles, and other items for daily living. The buffalo meat was their main source of food while the bones and horns were used to make tools.

Today there are only two tribes left in Texas. The Tigua Indians are found in the El Paso area and the Alabama Coushatta Indians have a reservation in east Texas. Many Indians died from European diseases or at the hands of the settlers who moved into Texas. The rest of the Indians have left or were moved to reservations in other states, mainly in Oklahoma.

©Plutarch Publications, Inc. PPI -4281

Spanish Explorers

The first known Spanish explorer, Alonso Alvarez de Pineda, came to Texas in 1519. Pineda was from Spain and explored the Texas coast looking for a good spot to start a colony. The settlement never came to be.

In 1528 a Spanish ship was wrecked in a hurricane along the Texas coast. Among the few survivors was a Spanish explorer named Alvar Nunez Cabeza de Vaca and a black slave named Estevanico. These two men were held captive by Karankawa Indians for several years. While they were prisoners they heard many tales about seven cities of gold. Vaca and Estevanico finally escaped and explored Texas on their way back to Mexico, but they never found any of the golden cities. Other Spaniards continued to come to Texas in search of these cities, exploring a large portion of Texas in the process. Spain was very disappointed that these early explorers did not find any gold, but because of these explorations they were able to claim Texas in the name of Spain. In 1682 Spanish priests founded two missions in what is now El Paso. Their main purpose was to teach Christianity to the Indians.

Alvar Nunex Cabeza de Vaca

During the 1680's the French became interested in exploring Texas. In 1685 a French explorer named Rene-Robert Cavalier, Sieur de La Salle, built a small fort near the Gulf Coast of Texas. This brought the French flag to Texas for the first time. The colony did not last long as starvation, disease, and Indian attacks took their toll. However, la Salle's explorations prompted the Spanish to settle Texas even more quickly.

In 1690 Mission San Francisco do los Tejas was built near what is now Houston. During the next sixty years, twenty more Spanish missions were built in Texas. In 1718 Mission San Antonio de Valero was built. This mission became the foundation for the city of San Antonio, the most important of the Spanish settlements in Texas. This mission later became known as the Alamo, a key place in Texas history. As missions spread across Texas, presidios (or forts) were built nearby. These missions and forts were the beginning of many major cities in Texas. The missions brought Spanish people and a new way of life to Texas.

During the 1700's many Spanish settlers moved northward from Mexico into Texas. Many of them brought horses to the area and set up cattle ranches. By the 1800's the French had abandoned Texas in favor of other areas of the New World. Without the pressure from the French, the Spanish once again lost interest in their drive to control this vast land known as Texas.

Name _____   Standard: History

American Settlers

During the late 1700's, the United States gained its independence from England. In 1803 the country bought the territory of Louisiana, bringing the United States boundaries up to the Texas line. People living near Texas became even more interested in this area. Between the years of 1820 and 1836 over 40,000 people from the United States came to Texas to settle. Texas was still under Spanish rule at the time.

Moses Austin was one of the first United States citizens to settle in Texas. He wanted to start a colony in this territory so he asked permission from the Spanish governor. In 1821 he was given permission to bring 300 United States families to Texas, but he died before he could carry out his plan. His son, Stephen, took over the effort.

During that same year (1821) Mexico became independent of Spain, and Texas was now under the Mexican flag. Stephen Austin, wanting to carry on with his father's work, made a new agreement with Mexico. He would be allowed to bring settlers to Texas, but they must become Mexican citizens and Roman Catholics. Austin returned to the United States and advertised for people wanting to move to Texas. He offered inexpensive land to law abiding citizens. Over the next ten years Austin brought about 6,000 United States citizens to Texas.

Austin was not the only one to receive permission for a colony in Texas. The idea of settling in an "untamed" land was exciting, and many people from the United States came to give it a try. Life in Texas was not easy for the new settlers. Men, women, and children had to work very hard and had little free time. The threat of Indian raids was always there. Droughts made it impossible for farmers to grow anything. At other times there was too much rain, or seeds were not available to plant. Even though life was difficult, few colonists gave up and returned to the United States. Most of them endured the hardships and made a living as best they could. By 1836 the population in Texas had grown to about 50,000.

1. Which country controlled Texas when Stephen Austin began the new colony?

_____

Give two reasons why life in Texas was difficult for new settlers:

2. _____
3. _____

Mexico asked Stephen Austin to make settlers agree to do what two things?

4. _____
5. _____

Name _____   Standard: History

The Revolution

In 1830 the Mexican government was not happy with the American way of life. This resulted in the Law of April 6, 1830, which brought new rules to the settlers. Americans would no longer be allowed to move to Texas, and those already settled there would have to return to the United States. Texas could no longer trade with American businesses and Americans would have to pay a tax to the Mexican government on anything they brought into Texas. These new rules did not make the settlers very happy!

in 1833, after the settlers had met and written a list of requests for the Mexican government, Stephen Austin traveled to Mexico City to meet with Mexican leaders. His visit was not successful, and he was thrown in jail before he could return. During his imprisonment the settlers did nothing to upset the Mexican government because they were afraid Austin would be hurt.

In 1833 Antonio Lopez de Santa Anna de Lebron (Santa Anna), a general in the Mexican army, became president of Mexico. In 1835 he sent Mexican troops to collect taxes from the Texans. He also began to take away more of their rights. Many of the Texans from the United States did not like what was happening so they organized a group (led by William Travis) to drive the Mexican troops away. This act marked the beginning of battle between Mexico and Texas. The first fight took place on October 2, 1835 in Gonzalez when the Mexican forces were driven back. Shortly after that the Texans captured the cities of Goliad and San Antonio.

Many Texans believed they were free from Mexico when they drove the army out of San Antonio. Many of the settlers returned to their homes, leaving only a few men and some supplies behind. However, Santa Anna was very angry and he sent troops back to San Antonio. When the Mexicans arrived in the city, the remaining Texans took refuge in the mission called the Alamo. On February 23, 1836 Santa Anna's troops began a 13 day attack on the Alamo. There were 189 Texans, led by William Travis, fighting against 5,000 Mexican soldiers. It did not take very long before the Texans were low on gun powder and supplies, but they refused to give in. In the early morning hours of March 6, three columns of Mexican troops rushed the Alamo. In less than two hours of battle, all the Texans were dead along with 600 Mexican soldiers.

During the battle at the Alamo, Texan leaders were meeting and they issued the Texas Declaration of Independence. Sam Houston was asked to lead the army. He immediately returned to Gonzalez to pick up his soldiers and head for the Alamo, but before he could bring help he learned that the Alamo had been defeated.

On March 27, Santa Anna ordered the death of 350 Texan soldiers taken in Goliad. On April 21, 1836 Sam Houston's army surprised Santa Anna and his troops at the Battle of San Jacinto. This battle marked the end of the war and Texas became an independent republic at last.

Name _____   Standard: History

Who Am I?
Read each description on the right and decide who it describes.
Write the letter of the correct person or group on each line.

A. Caddo

B. Comanche

C. de Pineda

D. de Vaca

E. Jumanos

F. Karankawa

G. La Salle

H. Sam Houston

I. Santa Anna

J. Stephen Austin

K. Tigua

L. William Travis

_____ An Indian tribe that lived along the coast and loved dogs.

_____ West Texas Indians who grew corn and hunted buffalo.

_____ This tribe called themselves "Tashas", or friends.

_____ Indian nomads and horse riders who relied on the buffalo for their survival.

_____ One of two Indian tribes remaining in Texas today.

_____ The first known Spanish explorer to come to Texas.

_____ He was taken prisoner and heard about seven golden cities in Texas.

_____ The first French explorer to colonize Texas.

_____ A colonizer who brought 300 families from the United States to settle in Texas.

_____ A Mexican general who became president.

_____ He led the Texans at the Alamo.

_____ He led the Texan army that defeated Santa Anna at San Jacinto.

©Plutarch Publications, Inc. PPI-4281

Name _____   Standard: History

Joining the Union

After the 1836 war against Mexico, Texas became an independent country named the Republic of Texas. Sam Houston became the first president of this country as it raised a new flag and issued its own money. Both the flag and the money were designed around one star, so the country quickly became known as the "Lone Star Republic". Life as an independent country had its problems as Texas struggled with disputes over establishing a border with Mexico, experienced Indian wars, and suffered financial problems. Many Texans, including Sam Houston, wanted to become a state of the United States. In September 1836, Texas voted to join the union. It was not quickly accepted by Congress, however, because Texas allowed slavery. Many of the early settlers had come from southern states and brought their slaves with them. Most of the northern states were against slavery and were not eager to have another state that allowed it. The debate in Congress continued for nine years, but Texas was admitted to the union as the 28th state on December 29, 1845.

The border disputes with Mexico had become a big problem. In 1846 (only a few months after Texas joined the union) the United States and Mexico went to war. The U.S. victory in 1848 established the Rio Grande as the border between the two counties. Texas claimed all the land along the Rio Grande as far as southern Colorado. Their new territory included what today is half of New Mexico and parts of Colorado, Wyoming, Oklahoma, and Kansas. The northern states were against expanding Texas because they did not want slavery to be allowed in the new territory. In the Compromise of 1850, Texas agreed to give up its claim to those lands in exchange for ten million dollars. By 1850, the population of Texas was 212,000. It tripled in the next ten years, rising to 600,000 by 1860.

1. What was the name of the independent country that Texas became in 1836?
   _____

2. Why was this country nicknamed the "Lone Star Republic"?
   _____

3. Why wasn't Texas immediately accepted as a state when it applied in 1836?
   _____

4. After the war with Mexico, Texas owned part of five other states. Name them.
   4. _____   7. _____
                             6. _____
   5. _____   8. _____

Name _____   Standard: History

The Civil War

    Slavery was allowed in Texas as well as many other southern states. The slaves were put to work in the cotton fields on large farms called plantations. The northern states were against slavery and wanted to put an end to the practice of buying and selling other human beings. In November of 1860 Abraham Lincoln, a man against slavery, was elected president of the United States. The southern states were not pleased with Lincoln and during the next few months they began to secede, or leave, the union of the United States. On February 1, 1861 Texas joined the south and became the seventh state to secede. Four other states seceded after Texas, bringing the total up to eleven. These states formed a new union called the Confederate States of America and they chose Jefferson Davis as their president.

    In April of 1861 the Civil War (also called The War Between the States) began. This was a war between the now divided northern and southern states. Very few battles of this war were fought on Texas soil. The most important battles in Texas were those fought over Galveston, a seaport city important to the South for trading and bringing in supplies. The last battle of the Civil War was fought in south Texas at Palmito Hill. The Confederate States won this battle, but what they didn't know was that the war was already over. The North had beaten the South a month earlier but the news had not reached the soldiers at Palmito Hill.

    After the Civil War there was a period of rebuilding homes, lives, and the country itself. This time was called the Reconstruction. The Confederate States rejoined the Union, but they were no longer allowed to own slaves. Reconstruction was not an easy time for people in Texas. The slaves were happy to be free, but most of them no longer had a home and could not find jobs. Many people had lost their land and money during the war. Families had been torn apart over their beliefs in which side was right. Texas, along with other states in the south, was soon over run with carpetbaggers (Northerners who moved to the South and entered politics during reconstruction). The carpetbaggers' aim was to become powerful in the government and get rich from the people as they struggled to recover from their loses in the war. Southerners exposed these cheats and forced them to move back north or get out of politics completely.

    On March 30, 1870 Texas was readmitted to the Union. Cattle ranching quickly grew as it became very important to the Texas economy. Huge herds of cattle were driven up the Chisholm Trail to Kansas where the railroad could easily ship them to other states. Many people wanted or needed the beef and leather from cattle, and Texas supplied the best that could be found. Slowly Texas began to recover from the scars of the Civil War.

©Plutarch Publications, Inc. PPI -4281

Name _____

Standard: History

Find the Facts

1. In what month and year did Texas first vote to join the Union?
   _____

2. Why did it take nine years for Texas to be admitted to the Union?
   _____
   _____

3. What river became the border between Texas and Mexico in the year 1848?
   _____

4. On what date did Texas secede from the Union? _____

5. Who was Jefferson Davis? _____
   _____

6. The most important Civil War battles fought in Texas were over which city? Why?
   _____
   _____

7. What was Reconstruction?
   _____

8. Which resource helped Texas recover from the economic loses after the war?
   _____

The following statements refer to either the North or South during the Civil War. Write "**N**" on the blank if it is about the North and "**S**" if it is about the South.

_____ It was called the Union.
_____ Lincoln was the president.
_____ They lost the war.
_____ Won the battle at Palmito Hill.
_____ Wanted to capture Galveston to cut off supplies imported there.
_____ Jefferson Davis was the president.
_____ Carpetbaggers were from here.
_____ Eleven states that seceded because they wanted to keep slavery.

Name _____

Standard: History

The Frontier

After the Civil War, Texans were hopeful that the Union army would help them fight the Indians that continued to raid settlements. The Indians depended on the buffalo for their survival. They used nearly every part of the animal to provide themselves with food, clothing, shelter, weapons, and tools. As more settlers came to Texas they shot buffalo for the hides, often leaving the rest of the animal to rot. By 1880 most of the buffalo were gone and the Indians were struggling to survive. They resented the settlers and raided in an effort to drive them off the land.

The United States government sent troops to the west to protect settlers and they began to make treaties with the Indians, encouraging them to become farmers. The Indians had always been hunters and farming was not something many of them enjoyed. After years of small battles and raids, most of the Indians were moved to areas of land called reservations. Most of these reservations were in Oklahoma. Buffalo herds were gone, no longer eating the grasslands and Indian raids were no longer a threat to the settlers. The land was suitable for grazing so many more cattle were brought into Texas. So began the time of cattle drives and cowboys of the west.

The development of these huge cattle ranches in Texas created a need for men to look after them. Most cowboys were southern soldiers from the Civil War that were looking for work. About one third of them were African-Americans or Mexican-Americans. They worked long and hard, often twenty hours a day, and were paid between 25 and 40 dollars a month. The cowboys learned the Spanish style of ranching, from handling cattle to types of equipment, that was commonly used in northern Mexico. The two most important jobs of the Texas cowboy were roundups and drives.

Roundups were events held mostly in the spring, but sometimes in the fall as well. The cattle from the ranch were "rounded up", or brought into one area of the ranch, to be sorted and branded. During the spring roundups cattle would be chosen to be taken to market and sold. These cattle must be taken to market in Kansas where they could be shipped by railroad to other states.

During the summer cattle drives were made, walking huge herds across the country to Kansas. The easiest route was the Chisholm Trail. Between 1865 and 1880 over three and a half million cattle were driven 1,500 to 3,000 miles along this trail to Kansas. The cowboys had to keep the herds together, see that they got water, guard them against predators and rustlers, and prevent stampedes. It was extremely difficult and lonely work.

By 1890 the railroads had expanded into many areas of Texas. The long drives to market were no longer necessary. Ranchers began to fence in their ranges, making it easier to keep track of their herds. The time of the cattle drives and "real" cowboys was slowly coming to an end.

©Plutarch Publications, Inc. PPI -4281

Name _____   Standard: History

The Twentieth Century

In 1901 the first huge oil deposit was discovered near Beaumont, Texas. Hundreds of oil workers arrived in Texas as more oil wells were developed. Oil was discovered almost everywhere they drilled, and Texas was booming. Industry and manufacturing began to grow and thrive in Texas as lumber, cotton, and oil brought jobs and money to the state. By 1928 Texas had become the top oil producing state in the country.

In 1929 the country entered a time known as the Great Depression. This was a time of great hardship for people every where. Industries were producing more products than they were able to sell. People lost their jobs, industries shut down, and no one could find work. This period lasted about ten years as the whole country suffered. The oil industry helped Texas survive these tough times. The economy began to improve in the early 1940's and then the United States entered World War II.

Jobs were once again plentiful across the country. People were needed to build airplanes, ships, and other things used in the war. Many American soldiers were trained at the bases in Texas. Most important to Texas was that large amounts of oil were needed to be used for fuel and other products. Over half of the oil used by the United States during World War II came from Texas. The oil industry was once again providing money for the state.

Texas Today

With a population of about 17 million people, Texas has more citizens than any state except California. The rural areas increased rapidly in the 1800's, but currently the urban areas are the fastest growing. Texas has the third largest African-American population and the second largest Hispanic population. The rest of the population comes from various nationalities.

This wonderful mix of cultural backgrounds provides for numerous festivities around the state. One of these is the well known Texas Folklife Festival in San Antonio. At this festival 27 ethnic groups share their culture and customs. Native clothing is worn while native arts and crafts are displayed.

Texas has several hundred libraries, the largest of which is at the University of Texas at Austin. There are over 300 museums, three major symphony orchestras, ballet companies, and two operas serving the fine arts needs of the state.

©Plutarch Publications, Inc. PPI -4281

Name _____   Standard: History Graphics

Flags over Texas

There have been six flags flown over Texas during its history.
Find each flag and paste or draw a picture in the appropriate box below.

Spain : 1519 to 1821

France : 1685 and 1690

Mexico : 1821 to 1836

Republic of Texas : 1836-1845

Confederacy : 1861 to 1865

United States of America :
1845 to 1861;
and 1865 to present.

©Plutarch Publications, Inc. PPI -4281

Name _____   Standard: History Graphics

History Time Line

Fill in the time line below by writing the correct name of each country on the line below the years its flag flew over Texas.

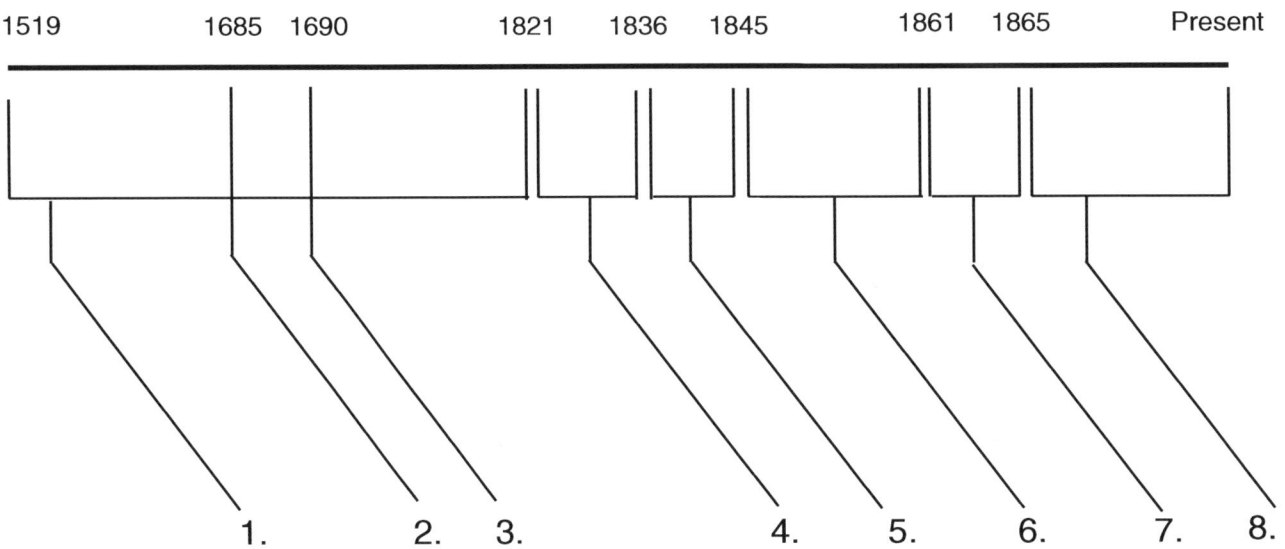

Answer the questions about these times in Texas history.

9. Which flag has flown over Texas for the longest time?
_____

Which countries had their flags over Texas twice?
10. _____   11. _____

What two countries flew their flag in Texas at the same time?
12. _____   13. _____

In which two years was Texas admitted to the Union?
14. _____   15. _____

16. How many years did the Confederate flag fly over Texas?
_____

17. How many years did Mexico control Texas?
_____

18. What country was the first to fly its flag in Texas?
_____

19. For which years did Texas fly her own flag as an independent country?
_____

©Plutarch Publications, Inc. PPI-4281

Name _____   Standard: History Graphics

Texas Time Line

A time line helps show historical events in the order in which they happened. Below is a time line showing the sequence of events leading to Texas becoming a state.

1519	Spanish explore and claim Texas
1685	French explore and claim parts of Texas
1718	The Alamo is built
1821	Mexico claims Texas
1836	Population is 50,000 and Texas becomes a Republic
1845	Texas becomes 28th State
1860	Population 600,000
1861	Texas joins the South and secedes
1870	Texas rejoins the Union
1890	Railroads end cattle drives
1901	Oil is discovered
1990	Population is 17 million

Use the time line to answer the questions below.

1. What was the population of Texas in 1836? _____

2. In what year did the railroad expansion affect the cattle drives? _____

3. In which years was Texas claimed by either Spain or France? _____

4. How much larger was the population in 1860 than in 1836? _____

5. What important event happened in Texas in 1901? _____

6. In what year did Texas become a republic? _____

7. In what year did the Civil War begin? _____

8. In what year was the Alamo built? _____

Activity: Make a time line of the important events in your life. You may use pictures or drawings to make your time line more personal.

©Plutarch Publications, Inc. PPI -4281

Name _____   Standard: History

Cause and Effect

Match the causes on the left with the effect they created on the right by putting the correct letter on the line.

_____ The American settlers in Texas were unhappy with Santa Anna's new taxes (Law of April 6, 1830).

_____ Mexican troops attacked the Alamo.

_____ Santa Anna was defeated at the Battle of San Jacinto.

_____ Abraham Lincoln, who opposed slavery, was elected President.

_____ Arguments developed over the border between Mexico and the new State of Texas.

_____ Settlers killed buffalo for the hides.

_____ Oil was discovered in Texas.

_____ Railroads came to many parts of Texas.

_____ The Great Depression hit the whole country.

A. The war between Mexico and the United States began in 1846.

B. Texans became an independent republic.

C. Texas seceded from the Union.

D. This created new jobs and money for Texans.

E. Austin went to Mexico City to meet with leaders and was taken prisoner.

F. Indians, struggling to survive, tried to drive away the settlers.

G. It was a time of hardship and many people lost their jobs.

H. Ranges were fenced and cattle drives were no longer necessary.

I. 189 Texans were killed at the San Antonio mission.

Fact or Opinion?

Write an "**F**" if the statement is fact and an "**O**" if it is opinion.

_____ Texas is the second largest state in the country.
_____ The pioneer women worked too hard.
_____ The battle of the Alamo should never have been fought.
_____ The Civil War was a battle between the North and the South.
_____ It was mean of the settlers to kill all the buffalo.
_____ Cattle ranching and oil have helped the economy of Texas to grow.

©Plutarch Publications, Inc. PPI-4281

Name _____

Standard: Review

Texas History

Read the clues below and give the name of what it describes.
Circle the names in the word search. They may go in any direction.

S	O	N	C	S	O	N	A	M	U	J	I
A	A	M	O	M	E	X	I	C	O	N	F
N	S	U	A	T	L	L	G	J	D	V	N
T	Y	D	G	L	S	T	U	E	U	N	L
A	R	D	U	I	A	U	P	A	Q	O	O
A	E	B	T	Z	T	E	O	W	K	W	C
N	V	P	W	P	N	A	S	H	I	X	N
N	A	J	J	D	U	O	N	I	M	E	I
A	L	T	E	S	D	I	R	X	V	A	L
E	S	N	T	D	A	L	W	M	R	A	S
Q	C	I	A	P	E	D	E	C	E	S	D
E	N	C	S	L	A	S	A	L	L	E	H

CLUES

1. A mission built in San Antonio in 1718. _____
2. An Indian tribe that had female chiefs. _____
3. Farming Indians in western Texas. _____
4. One of two Indian tribes remaining in Texas. _____
5. The first Frenchman to raise the French flag over Texas in 1685. _____
6. What the Texans won when they defeated Santa Anna. _____
7. The man who was the "Father of Texas". _____
8. The President of Mexico in 1833. _____
9. The first President of the Republic of Texas. _____
10. One issue that helped cause the Civil War. _____
11. The man who was President of the Union in 1861. _____
12. The man who was President of the Confederacy in 1861. _____
13. A word that means "to pull away or separate". _____
14. The country that is south of Texas. _____
15. The first country to claim the area later known as Texas. _____

Name _____   Standard: Famous Figures

Famous Texans

    The rich history of Texas brings to mind several well known figures. Two early heroes, David Crockett and Samuel Houston, were born in Tennessee but became famous in Texas. David Crockett (1786-1836) moved to Texas just one year before he died. He is best remembered as a defender of the Alamo who died there while fighting for the independence of Texas. Samuel Houston settled in Texas in 1835. He became the leader of the Texas army that defeated Santa Anna's army. Houston was the President of the Republic of Texas and later became a U.S. Senator. From 1859 to 1861 he served at the Governor of Texas.

    Many well known politicians have also been associated with the state. Two former Presidents of the United States were born in Texas. Dwight D. Eisenhower, a World War II general, was born in Denison. He was elected as the 34th President and held office from 1953 until 1961. Lyndon Johnson, born near Stonewall, was John F. Kennedy's Vice President. In 1963 Kennedy was assassinated and Johnson became the 36th President, serving office until 1969.

    George Bush was born in Massachusetts but moved to Texas in 1948. He made his fortune in the Texas oil industry. Bush became the Vice President under Ronald Regan and in 1989 was elected at the 41st President. His son, George Bush Jr., was elected Governor of Texas in 1994 and became the 43rd President in 2001.

    Barbara Jordan was born in Houston in 1936. She was the first woman and the first African-American in the Texas Senate, serving from 1966 to 1972. Jordan was a consultant to President Johnson for many civil rights issues. In 1973 she became the first southern African-American woman elected to the U.S. House of Representatives. She held that position until 1979.

    Henry Cisneros, another famous politician, was born in San Antonio in 1947. In 1981 he became the first Mexican-American in this country to be elected mayor of a major city. Under President Bill Clinton, Cisneros served at Secretary of Housing and Urban Development.

    Many famous athletes were born in Texas. Lee Trevino, a professional golfer, was born in Dallas in 1939. Nolan Ryan, a professional baseball player holding many records as pitcher, was born in Refugio in 1947. The famous race-car driver A. J. Foyt was born in Houston in 1935. In 1938 another race-car champion named Johnny Rutherford was born in Fort Worth. Willie Shoemaker, the jockey who has won more horse races than any other, was born in Fabens in 1931.

    These people, like the many other famous and not so famous faces in Texas, are part of what makes this huge state proud of what it has accomplished during its colorful and long history.

©Plutarch Publications, Inc. PPI-4281

Name _____   Standard: Review

Across

2. I moved to Texas just one year before I was killed at the Alamo.

6. I was the 41st President who made my money in Texas oil.

7. I was a race-car driver born in Fort Worth.

9. I am a professional golfer.

12. I was the 36th President of the United States.

Down

1. I was the President of the Republic of Texas.

3. I was the 34th President of the United States.

4. I am the jockey who has won more horse races than any other jockey.

5. I am a racecar diver born in Houston in 1935.

8. I served as Secretary of Housing and Urban Development under Bill Clinton.

10. I am a professional baseball pitcher.

11. I was the first woman elected to the Texas Senate in 1966.

©Plutarch Publications, Inc. PPI -4281

Name _____   Standard: Review

Review Crossword Clues

Across

2. The colors on the Texas flag are red, white, and _____.
3. A group of Indians that called themselves "tayshas", or friends were _____.
9. This man was a Mexican general and President.
10. This man brought over 300 families to settle in Texas
11. "The Father of Texas" was _____ F. Austin.
13. Six of these _____ flew over Texas during its history.
14. The large body of water to the southeast of Texas is the _____ of Mexico.
18. The first known Spanish explorer to come to Texas was _____.
19. The city in western Texas just across the river from Juarez, Mexico is _____.
22. Texas joined the _____ States when it seceded in 1861.
24. The _____ States was the country that Texas became part of in 1845.
25. The mockingbird is _____ and white.
27. The second largest state in the United States is _____.
28. The river that separates Texas from Mexico is the _____.
29. _____ is the state gem.

Down

1. The white panel on the Texas flag stands for _____.
3. Texas supplies meat from their herds of _____ .
4. The red panel on the Texas flag stands for _____.
5. The olive branch on the Seal of Texas symbolizes _____.
6. Texas is also known as the _____ _____ state.
7. Texas seceded from the _____ in 1861.
8. This city hosts the Cotton Bowl on New Years Day.
9. The live oak branch on the State Seal stands for _____.
12. The _____ river separates Louisiana and Texas.
13. The flag of _____ flew over Texas in 1685 and 1690.
15. The first flag to fly over Texas was from this country.
16. This body of water separates Texas and Oklahoma.
17. The Astrodome and Johnson Space Center are in or near the city of _____.
20. The blue panel on the Texas flag stands for _____.
21. The flag of _____ flew over Texas from 1821 to 1836.
23. The _____ of Texas lasted from 1836 to 1845.
26. The mission built in 1718 in San Antonio was the _____.

©Plutarch Publications, Inc. PPI -4281

Name _____ Standard: Review

Name _____

Standard: Review

Fact or Opinion?

Write an "**F**" if the statement is fact and an "**O**" if it is opinion.

_____ 1. Texas is the best state in which to live.
_____ 2. Texas has a population of about 24 million.
_____ 3. The Mexicans were wrong to attack the Alamo.
_____ 4. Eastern Texas is the prettiest part of the state.
_____ 5. Guadalupe Peak is the highest point in Texas.
_____ 6. Eighty percent of the population lives in urban areas.
_____ 7. The country is a nicer place to live than the city.
_____ 8. The bluebonnet is the most beautiful flower that grows wild in Texas.
_____ 9. The State Seal has olive and oak branches around the star.
_____ 10. The mockingbird is white and gray.
_____ 11. The mockingbird makes lovely mimicking noises.
_____ 12. Pecan trees grow very well in Texas forests.
_____ 13. Pecans are the most delicious nuts.
_____ 14. Austin is the best place to hear live music.
_____ 15. The Cotton Bowl is always played in Dallas.
_____ 16. The Alamo is in San Antonio.
_____ 17. El Paso is the Spanish Term for "the pass".
_____ 18. Twenty-one percent of the Texas population is Hispanic.
_____ 19. The mountains and basins region has the most spectacular sights in Texas.
_____ 20. Oil is the best investment anyone can make.
_____ 21. Cattle now graze where buffalo once did.
_____ 22. Spain was the first country to raise its flag over Texas.
_____ 23. Lyndon Johnson was a great President.
_____ 24. Corpus Christi is the nicest resort area.
_____ 25. The state gem is the topaz.
_____ 26. The State Capital Building is made of pink granite.
_____ 27. Austin is the capital of Texas.
_____ 28. Texas raises the best cattle meat in the country.
_____ 29. The Comanche and Apache tribes were nomads and great fighters.
_____ 30. Using a time line is the best way to study Texas history.

©Plutarch Publications, Inc. PPI-4281

Name _____   Standard: Review

Texas

Read the clues below and give the name of what it describes.
Circle the names in the word search. They may go in any direction.

I	N	Y	R	E	V	A	R	B	S	E	B	A
X	T	A	L	E	F	I	R	X	C	D	U	A
O	D	S	C	I	K	R	E	A	R	S	S	S
L	P	N	I	E	O	T	E	I	T	V	T	T
L	U	N	A	R	P	P	B	I	X	S	R	R
I	R	F	B	L	H	G	N	F	B	A	E	O
R	I	Y	Y	T	N	C	E	O	T	X	N	D
A	T	S	O	I	C	D	S	L	F	E	G	O
M	Y	P	K	I	Q	A	A	U	T	T	T	M
A	A	C	T	V	V	T	E	L	P	T	H	E
Z	O	R	E	L	P	A	S	O	L	R	A	J
M	U	H	I	S	P	A	N	I	C	A	O	C
S	B	L	U	E	B	O	N	N	E	T	S	C

CLUES

1. The state bird. _____
2. The state gem. _____
3. The olive branch on the State Seal symbolizes this. _____
4. The oak branch on the State Seal symbolizes this. _____
5. Home of the Cowboys football team. _____
6. The state tree. _____
7. The state flower. _____
8. What the color red symbolizes on the state flag. _____
9. What the color white symbolizes on the state flag. _____
10. The capital city. _____
11. The 28th state to join the United States. _____
12. The city where helium is produced. _____
13. A busy port city on the Gulf of Mexico. _____
14. The natural resource discovered in 1901. _____
15. Herds of these were once driven up the Chisholm Trail. _____
16. 80% of this resource is used for ranching and farming. _____
17. This group of fruits are grown in southern Texas. _____
18. A large city in western Texas. _____
19. 21% of the population is made of this ethnic group. _____
20. This arena is located in Houston. _____

Name _____ Standard: Comprehension

UNIT TEST

Part I
Read the statements and decide whether each is true or false.
On the blank, put 'T" if the statement is true and "O" if it is false.

_____ 1. A star is at the center of the State Seal of Texas.
_____ 2. Texas became a state in 1845.
_____ 3. The state nickname is "Friendship".
_____ 4. The Texas state flower is the daisy.
_____ 5. The Spanish flag was the third one to be flown over Texas.
_____ 6. Lyndon Johnson was not born in Texas, but he lived there most of his life.
_____ 7. The Texas state capital building is made of pink granite.
_____ 8. The Alamo was built near Houston.
_____ 9. Santa Anna was a Mexican general and president.
_____ 10. Texas is the second largest state in the country.

Part II
Write the correct answer for each blank.

11. The capital of Texas is _____
12. The nickname for Texas is _____
13. The state bird is _____
14. The olive branch on the State Seal of Texas stands for _____
15. The color blue on the state flag stands for _____

The four states that touch the Texas border are:

16. _____
17. _____
18. _____
19. _____
20. The body of water located southeast of Texas is _____
21. The river that separates Texas and Mexico is the _____

The four regions of Texas are :

22. _____
23. _____
24. _____
25. _____

©Plutarch Publications, Inc. PPI -4281

Name _____   Standard: Comprehension

Part III
Match each flag with the dates it flew over Texas.

_____ 26. The Confederate flag   A. 1861-1865
_____ 27. The French flag   B. 1685 and 1690
_____ 28. The Mexican flag   C. 1836-1845
_____ 29. The Republic of Texas flag   D. 1845-1861; 1865 to present
_____ 30. The Spanish flag   E. 1821-1836
_____ 31. The United States flag   F. 1519-1821

Part IV
Short answer

32. Name the state tree. _____

Name the two leading economic resources of Texas:

33. _____
34. _____
35. What does the live oak branch on the State Seal stand for? _____
36. What river lies between Texas and Louisiana? _____
37. In which city would you find the Astrodome? _____
38. Which city is known as the "Live Music Capital of the World"? _____
39. Which city is also known as "The Alamo City"? _____
40. Where is the Cotton Bowl held every year? _____
41. The name of the area excellent for growing citrus fruits? _____
42. Which city is the world's largest producer of helium? _____
43. Where is "Tornado Alley" located? _____
44. Which city lies across the Rio Grande from Juarez, Mexico? _____
45. The name of which city comes from the Spanish word for yellow? __
46. Name the region of Texas where the "Piney Woods" is found: _____
47. Which region in west Texas has most of the mountains? _____
48. Which port city was important to Texas during the Civil War? ____
49. Palo Duro canyon is just outside which city? _____
50. What animal was brought in after the buffalo were gone? _____

©Plutarch Publications, Inc. PPI -4281

Name _____   Standard: Comprehension

Part V
Read the statements and decide whether each is true or false.
On the blank, put "**T**" if the statement is true and "**O**" if it is false.

_____ 51. Texas seceded from the Union during the war with Mexico.
_____ 52. The state bird is the mockingbird.
_____ 53. The name Texas came from the Spanish word "tejas" for friends.
_____ 54. Most of the Texan population lives in the rural areas.
_____ 55. Texas was the 20th state to join the Union.
_____ 56. Texas joined the Union on December 29, 1845.
_____ 57. The white panel on the state flag stands for purity.
_____ 58. The words "The Lone Star State" appear on the State Seal.
_____ 59. The bluebonnet is a beautiful purple and pink flower.
_____ 60. Opals are the state gem.
_____ 61. Houston and San Antonio are in the top ten largest cities in the U.S.
_____ 62. The city of Austin was named for Stephen F. Austin.
_____ 63. Johnson Space Center is found near Houston.
_____ 64. Dallas is home of the professional football team called "Cowboys".
_____ 65. El Paso is in western Texas.
_____ 66. Mustang Island, a tourist spot, is located in the Red River.
_____ 67. El Paso is the Spanish term for "the pass".
_____ 68. More African-Americans live in Texas than do Hispanics.
_____ 69. All early cowboys were southern white soldiers from the Civil War.
_____ 70. Texas is often hit by hurricanes, tornadoes, and earthquakes.

Part VI
Multiple Choice. Circle the correct answer.

71. Oil was first discovered in Texas in:
    A. 1879   C. 1901
    B. 1899   D. 1921

72. Texas has more inland water than any state except:
    A. Alabama   C. California
    B. Alaska   D. Michigan

73. This Indian tribe sometimes ate their captured enemies to gain their strength and courage.
    A. Caddo   C. Jumanos
    B. Comanche   D. Karankawa

Part VII
Match each place listed below with the number that represents it on the map.

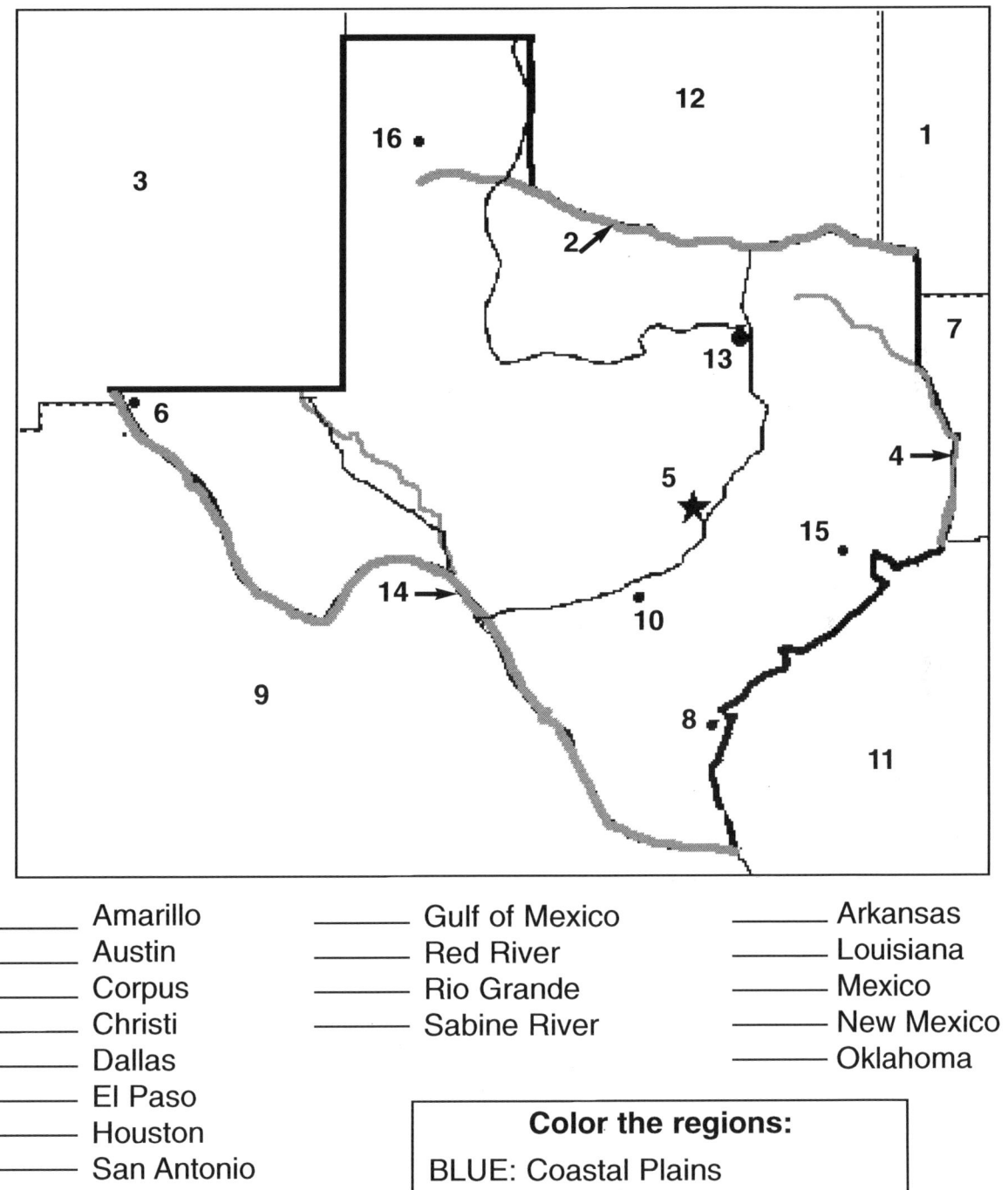

_____ Amarillo   _____ Gulf of Mexico   _____ Arkansas
_____ Austin   _____ Red River   _____ Louisiana
_____ Corpus   _____ Rio Grande   _____ Mexico
_____ Christi   _____ Sabine River   _____ New Mexico
_____ Dallas   _____ Oklahoma
_____ El Paso
_____ Houston
_____ San Antonio

Color the regions:

BLUE: Coastal Plains
GREEN: Great Plains
ORANGE: North Central Plains
BROWN: Mountains and Basins

Extension Activities

Symbols

Trace the history of the state seal and how it has changed since the territorial days.

What do the words union, justice, and confidence mean to you? Make a flag that could be used as a symbol of your class or school.

Major Cities

Research facts to write a one page article about your city or town. If your city or town was discussed in this book, what other important facts might you add?

Select a hobby or interest you have and find out if the state has any museums, parks, or festivals that support it. Present your findings in a report.

Geography

Record the temperature in your town or city for two weeks and make a line graph with your information.

History

What group of Indians were the original inhabitants in your area? What further information can you find on them?

What eleven states seceded from the Union and became the Confederacy? When was each of those states readmitted to the Union?

What does segregation mean? Give some modern day examples of segregation.

Graphics

Make a timeline that shows the important events in your life. You can use photos and draw pictures to illustrate the events.

Select ten cities in your state that you would like to visit. Survey thirty or more people and have them select their favorite place to visit. Graph the results to see which city is most popular as a local tourist attraction.

©Plutarch Publications, Inc. PPI -4281

ANSWER KEYS: 13, 14, 15, 16

Name _____   Standard: State Symbols

Find the Facts

1. What does the word "symbol" mean? **SYMBOLS ARE ITEMS, PICTURES, OR COLORS THAT REPRESENT IDEAS OR FEELINGS.**

2. What do the three colors on the Texas state flag represent?
   blue **LOYALTY**   white **PURITY**   red **BRAVERY**

3. Why was Texas nicknamed the "Lone Star State"? **THERE IS ONLY ONE STAR ON THE STATE FLAG.**

4. Where will you always see the State Seal? **THE STATE SEAL IS ON ALL GOVERNMENT OFFICES AND ON OFFICIAL STATE PAPERS.**

5. What do the olive and oak branches symbolize on the State Seal? **THE OAK SYMBOLIZES STRENGTH AND THE OLIVE MEANS PEACE.**

6. What words are found on the Texas State Seal? **"THE STATE OF TEXAS"**

7. In what year did the mockingbird become the State Bird of Texas? **1927**

8. What makes the mockingbird so unusual? **IT IS ABLE TO IMITATE MANY FAMILIAR SOUNDS.**

9. Why do you think the bluebonnet was chosen as the State Flower? **IT GROWS ALL OVER THE STATE.**

10. What is the State Tree of Texas? **PECAN TREE**

11. What products are made from the State Tree? **FURNITURE, FLOORING, AND OTHER WOOD PRODUCTS.**

12. What is the Texas State Gem? **TOPAZ**

Name _____   Standard: Major Cities

Austin: The Capital

In 1839 the village of Waterloo, built on the Colorado River in central Texas, was selected as the state capital. It was renamed Austin for Stephen F. Austin, sometimes called the Father of Texas. In 1842 Austin was under frequent raids from Mexicans and Indians, so the government offices were moved to Houston until they could return to Austin in 1845.

Austin is noted as an education center with the huge campus of University of Texas located there. It is also known as the "Live Music Capital of the World" with many live music clubs on famous Sixth Street. Austin is a beautiful city with broad, tree lined streets and hills rising from the river. It grew rapidly during the 1980's and has become a popular tourist city. A 2005 Census shows the metropolitan population to be 690,252 which makes it the 16th largest city in the United States. The climate for this area is mild with an average temperature of 68° and a yearly rainfall of 31 inches.

The state capital building, completed in 1888, sits on one of the hills rising up from the river. Land in western Texas was sold to pay for the new building. The nation's capital in Washington, D.C. was used as a model for the Texas capital building. It is made of pink granite that was taken from Marble Falls, Texas. The building covers three acres of land and has over eighteen acres of floor space.

1. Label Austin on the map.
   List three facts about the city of Austin. **Answers may vary**
2. **AUSTIN WAS NAMED FOR STEPHEN AUSTIN, THE "FATHER OF TEXAS".**
3. **THE CITY OF AUSTIN IS KNOWN AS AN EDUCATION CENTER.**
4. **AUSTIN IS CALLED THE "LIVE MUSIC CAPITAL OF THE WORLD".**
5. Of what stone is the Austin capital building made? **PINK GRANITE**
6. What was the original name of Austin? **WATERLOO.**
7. Why were the state offices moved to Houston in 1842? **FREQUENT INDIAN AND MEXICAN RAIDS CAUSED TEXANS TO MOVE THE CAPITAL**

Name _____   Standard: Major Cities

Houston and Dallas

Houston, the largest city in Texas and the third largest in the country, is located in southeast Texas. It was founded in 1836 and named for Sam Houston, a famous Texan. Houston was the capital of the Republic of Texas until was moved to Austin in 1845.

Houston, with a population of 2,009,690 (2003 Census) is a leading center for refining oil and producing chemicals. Although it is 80 km (50 mi.) from the Gulf of Mexico, a connecting waterway makes Houston the third busiest port in the country. Southeast of Houston is the Johnson Space Center. Astronauts are trained and mission control for all space flights are directed from here. Houston is also home of the Astrodome, the first domed stadium built in the United States.

Dallas, with a population of 1,208,318 (2005 Census), is the second largest city in the state. It is located on Trinity River prairie flats of northeastern Texas. It was founded in 1841 and was named for George Dallas, the Vice President of the United States at that time. During its early years Dallas was a cotton marketing center. Today that past is still remembered with the New Year's Day football game known as the "Cotton Bowl". Dallas has become a center for banking, insurance companies, and fashion design. It is the home of the professional football team the Dallas Cowboys and has one of the largest year round farmer's market in the nation. Ft. Worth, just to the west of Dallas, is so close the cities are called the Dallas/Ft. Worth area. Their combined population is about 4,000,000.

1. Label Houston and Dallas on the map.
2. Compare these two cities by filling in the chart below:

	Population	Founded	Named for	Location	Point of interest
Houston	2,009,690	1836	Sam Houston	southeast	Johnson Space Center
Dallas	1,208,318	1841	George Dallas	prairie flatlands	Cotton Bowl

---

Name _____   Standard: Major Cities

San Antonio

San Antonio, with a population of 1,256,509 (2005 Census) is the third largest city in Texas, and the 7th largest in the United States. It was founded in 1796 as a Spanish garrison (fort) with several small missions nearby. Early Spanish and Mexican pioneer families came to these missions to live and work. One mission, the Alamo, became an important battle site when Texas fought for its independence from Mexico in 1836. San Antonio was also located at the beginning of the Chisholm Trail, a famous trail for driving cattle from Texas to Kansas where they would be sold and shipped further east. Because of its rich history and Mexican/Spanish roots, the city has a very distinctive style of architecture and a unique culture which has made it a huge tourist attraction.

1. Label San Antonio on the map.
   List three facts about the city of San Antonio: **Answers may vary**
2. **SAN ANTONIO IS THE THIRD LARGEST CITY IN TEXAS.**
3. **IT IS THE HOME OF THE ALAMO.**
4. **SAN ANTONIO WAS AT THE HEAD OF THE CHISHOLM TRAIN.**
5. In what year was San Antonio founded? **1796.**
   What two nationalities originally settled in San Antonio?
   6. **SPANISH**   7. **MEXICAN**
8. Which mission in San Antonio became famous in 1836?
   THE ALAMO
   What two things found in San Antonio are unusual because of the blending of the Spanish and Mexican peoples?
   9. **ARCHITECTURE**   10. **CULTURE**

©Plutarch Publications, Inc. PPI-4281

ANSWER KEYS: 18, 19, 20, 21

Name _____ Standard: Major Cities

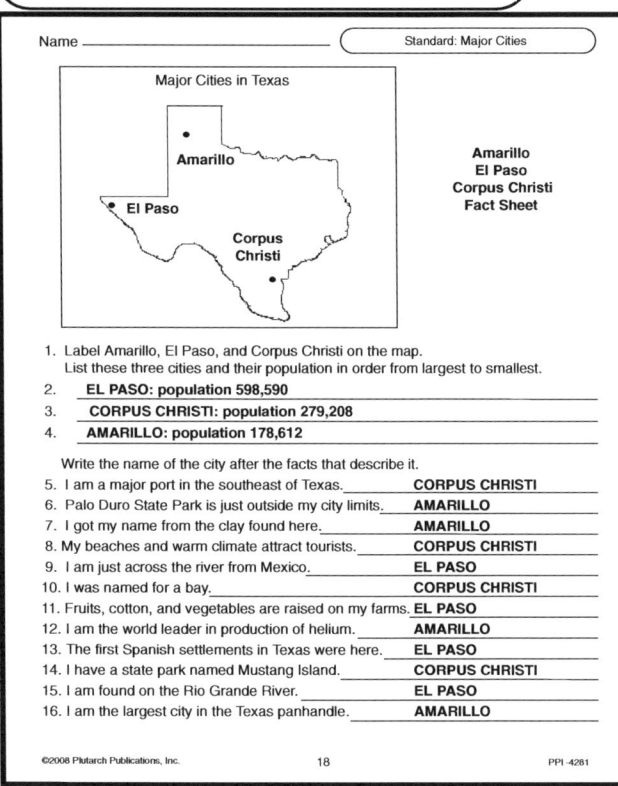

Major Cities in Texas

Amarillo
El Paso
Corpus Christi
Fact Sheet

1. Label Amarillo, El Paso, and Corpus Christi on the map.
   List these three cities and their population in order from largest to smallest.
2. **EL PASO: population 598,590**
3. **CORPUS CHRISTI: population 279,208**
4. **AMARILLO: population 178,612**

Write the name of the city after the facts that describe it.
5. I am a major port in the southeast of Texas. **CORPUS CHRISTI**
6. Palo Duro State Park is just outside my city limits. **AMARILLO**
7. I got my name from the clay found here. **AMARILLO**
8. My beaches and warm climate attract tourists. **CORPUS CHRISTI**
9. I am just across the river from Mexico. **EL PASO**
10. I was named for a bay. **CORPUS CHRISTI**
11. Fruits, cotton, and vegetables are raised on my farms. **EL PASO**
12. I am the world leader in production of helium. **AMARILLO**
13. The first Spanish settlements in Texas were here. **EL PASO**
14. I have a state park named Mustang Island. **CORPUS CHRISTI**
15. I am found on the Rio Grande River. **EL PASO**
16. I am the largest city in the Texas panhandle. **AMARILLO**

Name _____ Standard: Major Cities Graphics

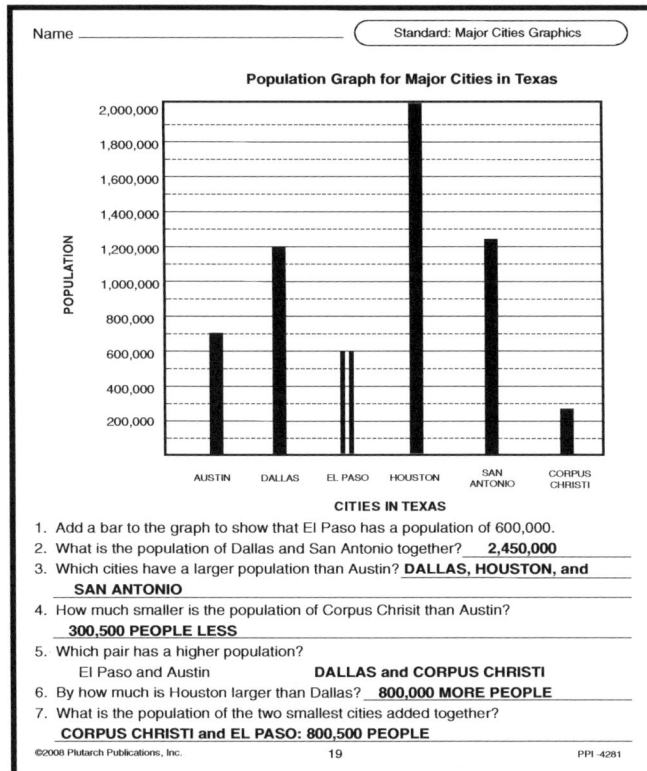

Population Graph for Major Cities in Texas

1. Add a bar to the graph to show that El Paso has a population of 600,000.
2. What is the population of Dallas and San Antonio together? **2,450,000**
3. Which cities have a larger population than Austin? **DALLAS, HOUSTON, and SAN ANTONIO**
4. How much smaller is the population of Corpus Chrisit than Austin? **300,500 PEOPLE LESS**
5. Which pair has a higher population?
   El Paso and Austin   **DALLAS and CORPUS CHRISTI**
6. By how much is Houston larger than Dallas? **800,000 MORE PEOPLE**
7. What is the population of the two smallest cities added together?
   CORPUS CHRISTI and EL PASO: 800,500 PEOPLE

Name _____ Standard: Major Cities Graphics

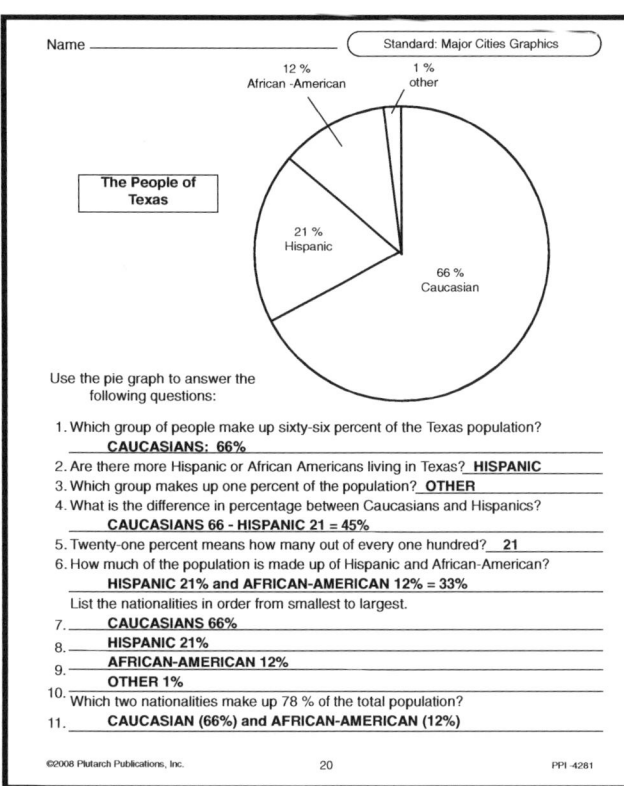

The People of Texas

Use the pie graph to answer the following questions:

1. Which group of people make up sixty-six percent of the Texas population?
   CAUCASIANS: 66%
2. Are there more Hispanic or African Americans living in Texas? **HISPANIC**
3. Which group makes up one percent of the population? **OTHER**
4. What is the difference in percentage between Caucasians and Hispanics?
   CAUCASIANS 66 - HISPANIC 21 = 45%
5. Twenty-one percent means how many out of every one hundred? **21**
6. How much of the population is made up of Hispanic and African-American?
   HISPANIC 21% and AFRICAN-AMERICAN 12% = 33%
   List the nationalities in order from smallest to largest.
7. **CAUCASIANS 66%**
8. **HISPANIC 21%**
9. **AFRICAN-AMERICAN 12%**
10. **OTHER 1%**
11. Which two nationalities make up 78% of the total population?
    CAUCASIAN (66%) and AFRICAN-AMERICAN (12%)

Name _____ Standard: Geography

Regions of Texas

Texas can be divided into four natural regions: the Coastal Plains in the east and southeast; the North Central Plains from the north to the center of the state; the Great Plains extending from north to south central; and the Mountains and Basins in the far southwest.

Close to one third of Texas is in the Coastal Plains region. This is the area that follows along the coast of the Gulf of Mexico and goes inland about 80 to 100 kilometers (50-60 miles). The Coastal Plains stretch across the rolling hilly lands of eastern Texas, including the forested lands in the northeast. The highest elevation (distance above sea level) is 150 meters (500 ft.). The western side of this region is a fertile belt of land called the Blackland Prairie. Houston, Dallas, Austin, San Antonio, and Corpus Christi are the largest cities in this region.

The North Central Plains region is mainly covered with farms and ranches. This region begins at the Oklahoma border and reaches south to about the middle of Texas. The land here is a little higher and more hilly than that of the Coastal Plains. Fort Worth, Arlington, and Abilene are the major cities in this region.

The Great Plains region covers a long strip extending from the northern tip of Texas to the border of Mexico. The lands in the Great Plains region are flat tablelands with an elevation of up to 1,200 meters (4,000 ft.). The region includes many areas with rich farm land. Major cities are Amarillo, Lubbock, Midland, and Odessa.

The region in the far southeastern corner of Texas is called the Mountains and Basins. The highest elevations in Texas are found here in the Guadalupe and Davis Mountains with the highest point at 2,667 meters (8,749 ft.). Rolling hills run along the Pecos River Valley. El Paso is the largest city in this region.

Use the information above to label the four regions of Texas on this map.

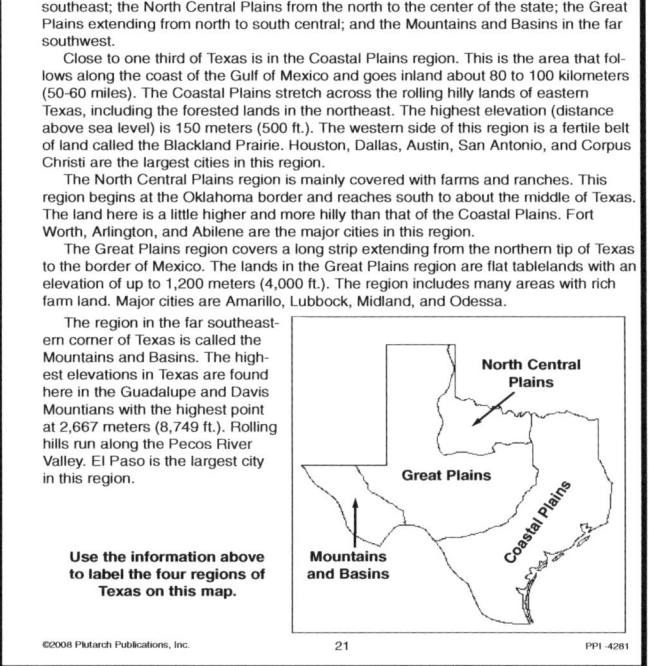

ANSWER KEYS: 22, 23, 25, 26

Page 22 — Climate

Texas has a broad range in climate. In southern Texas, summer temperatures can rise as high as 49° C (120°F) and do not usually go much lower than 20°C (50° F) in the winter months. However, winter temperatures in the west and northern parts of Texas can be much colder. For example, Amarillo (in the northern panhandle) gets snow every year and often has temperatures below freezing. Some areas may get as cold as -31° C (23° F) during the winter.

Precipitation, the amount of moisture that falls to earth, varies greatly across the state. An area in extreme west Texas receives an average of less than eight inches a year while parts of eastern Texas along the Sabine River average more than 59 inches per year.

Texas also has its share of floods, droughts, tornadoes, and hurricanes. Floods occur in many areas that are generally very dry. If large amounts of rain fall in a short period, the hardened ground cannot absorb the water fast enough and it quickly builds up to high levels. Droughts are long periods of dry weather with little or no precipitation. During droughts grasses die, causing the topsoil to turn to dust and blow away.

Texas is no stranger to the dangerous and sometimes deadly storm called the tornado. An average of one hundred tornadoes are sighted in Texas each year. The Red River Valley, an area that crosses northern Texas, has earned the nickname "Tornado Alley" because it is the frequent target of these storms. No other state is hit by as many tornadoes as Texas.

Hurricanes occur when tropical storms form over the warm waters of the Gulf of Mexico. As these tropical storms grow in size they may become hurricanes which sometimes hit the Texas coast. When these huge storms come ashore they can push water from the Gulf several miles inland. They begin to die as they continue over the land, dumping large amounts of rain over the area as they go. One of the most destructive hurricanes ever hit Galveston in 1900, killing over 6,000 people. Over the years forecasters have become very good at predicting where a hurricane will land, allowing people more time to move to safer areas.

What are the warmest and coolest temperatures of the Texas climate?
1. warmest __49°C (120° F)__   2. coolest __-31° C (23° F)__
3. In what year was Galveston hit by a deadly hurricane? __1900__

What is the average annual rainfall in eastern and western Texas?
4. eastern __59 inches__   5. western __8 inches__
6. What is a drought? __LONG, DRY PERIODS OF WEATHER__
7. What is the average number of tornadoes spotted in Texas per year? __100__
8. Which state reports more tornadoes than Texas? __NO OTHER STATE HAS MORE__

Page 23 — Average Fahrenheit Temperatures in Texas - Maximum/Minimum

	JAN.	FEB.	MAR.	APR.	MAY	JUNE	JULY	AUG.	SEPT.	OCT.	NOV.	DEC.
Amarillo	49 / 24	53 / 27	60 / 36	70 / 42	78 / 52	89 / 62	92 / 66	91 / 65	83 / 57	73 / 46	59 / 32	51 / 26
Austin	60 / 41	64 / 44	71 / 49	78 / 57	85 / 65	92 / 72	95 / 74	96 / 74	90 / 69	82 / 60	70 / 48	63 / 43
Corpus Christi	67 / 47	70 / 51	74 / 56	80 / 63	85 / 69	91 / 74	94 / 75	94 / 75	90 / 71	85 / 65	74 / 54	69 / 50
Dallas	56 / 36	60 / 39	67 / 45	75 / 55	83 / 63	91 / 72	95 / 75	95 / 75	88 / 67	79 / 57	66 / 44	58 / 38
El Paso	56 / 32	62 / 37	68 / 41	77 / 50	86 / 58	94 / 67	94 / 69	92 / 68	87 / 62	79 / 52	66 / 38	58 / 33
Houston	62 / 46	66 / 50	71 / 54	78 / 61	85 / 67	90 / 74	92 / 75	93 / 75	89 / 71	82 / 63	71 / 53	64 / 47
San Antonio	62 / 42	66 / 45	72 / 50	79 / 58	85 / 65	92 / 72	94 / 74	94 / 73	89 / 69	82 / 60	70 / 49	65 / 42

Use this table to answer the questions below.

1. Which city has the highest average temperature during the month of August? __AUSTIN 96°__
2. Give the difference in the low average between Amarillo and Houston in July: __9° difference__
3. El Paso's lowest high temperature is during what month? __JANUARY__
4. What are the two hottest months for Dallas? __JULY and AUGUST__
5. What two cities have the same average high in February? __HOUSTON and SAN ANTONIO__
6. How many months do Dallas and El Paso have the same average high temperature? __5__
7. What is the difference between the average high and low in El Paso during June? __94 - 67 = 27°__
8. What city has three months when the average low is below freezing? __AMARILLO__
9. In what month do Austin and Dallas have the same average low temperature? __JUNE 72°__
10. What is the warmest month for Austin? __AUGUST 96°__

Page 25 — Map of Important Cities and Areas in Texas

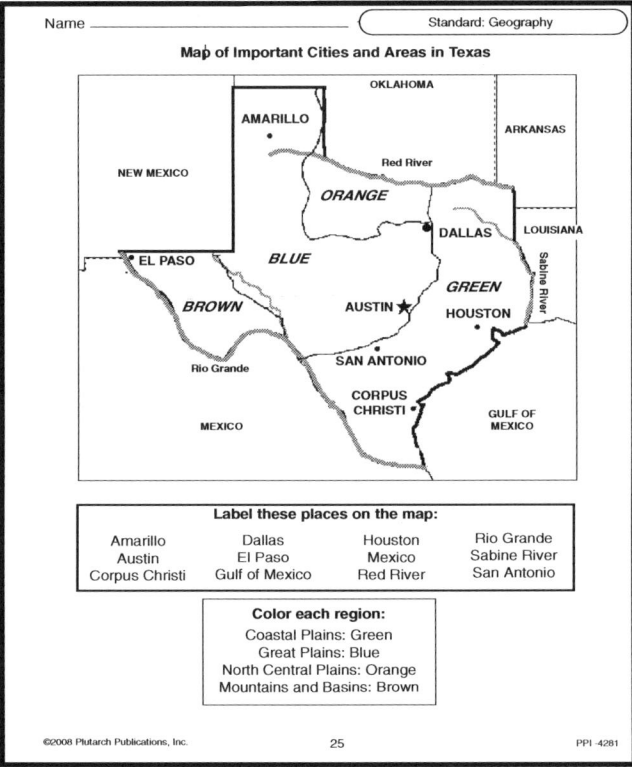

Label these places on the map:
Amarillo, Dallas, Houston, Rio Grande, Austin, El Paso, Mexico, Sabine River, Corpus Christi, Gulf of Mexico, Red River, San Antonio

Color each region:
Coastal Plains: Green
Great Plains: Blue
North Central Plains: Orange
Mountains and Basins: Brown

Page 26

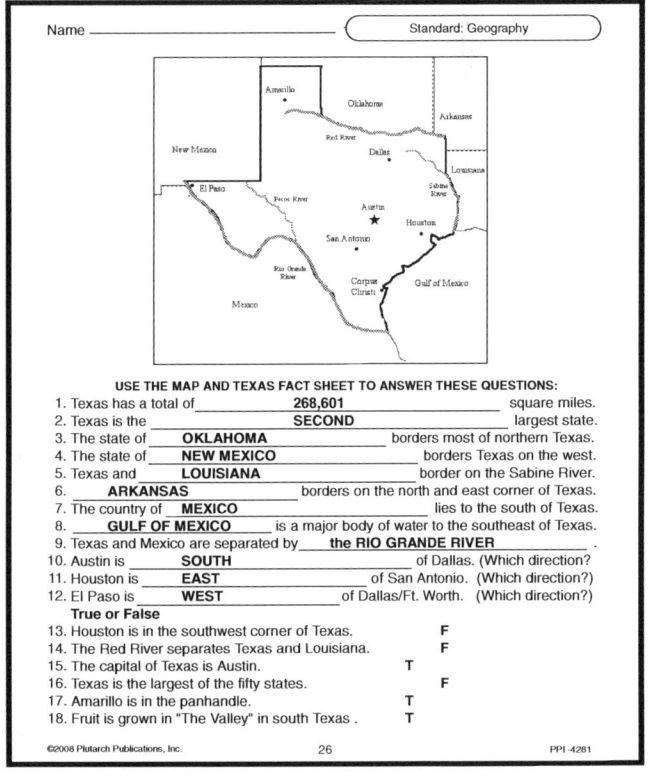

USE THE MAP AND TEXAS FACT SHEET TO ANSWER THESE QUESTIONS:
1. Texas has a total of __268,601__ square miles.
2. Texas is the __SECOND__ largest state.
3. The state of __OKLAHOMA__ borders most of northern Texas.
4. The state of __NEW MEXICO__ borders Texas on the west.
5. Texas and __LOUISIANA__ border on the Sabine River.
6. __ARKANSAS__ borders on the north and east corner of Texas.
7. The country of __MEXICO__ lies to the south of Texas.
8. __GULF OF MEXICO__ is a major body of water to the southeast of Texas.
9. Texas and Mexico are separated by __the RIO GRANDE RIVER__
10. Austin is __SOUTH__ of Dallas. (Which direction?)
11. Houston is __EAST__ of San Antonio. (Which direction?)
12. El Paso is __WEST__ of Dallas/Ft. Worth. (Which direction?)

True or False
13. Houston is in the southwest corner of Texas. __F__
14. The Red River separates Texas and Louisiana. __F__
15. The capital of Texas is Austin. __T__
16. Texas is the largest of the fifty states. __F__
17. Amarillo is in the panhandle. __T__
18. Fruit is grown in "The Valley" in south Texas. __T__

ANSWER KEYS: 28, 31, 33, 34

Name _____ **Standard: Review**

Quick Quiz

1. The city of Austin was named after what person?
   STEPHEN F. AUSTIN
2. In 1842, the capital of Texas was moved from Austin to what other city?
   HOUSTON
3. What stone is the Texas State Capital Building made of and from where was the stone taken?
   PINK GRANITE taken from MARBLE FALLS, TEXAS
4. For what famous person was the city of Houston named?
   SAM HOUSTON.
5. What famous sports arena is located in Houston?
   ASTRODOME
6. The city of Dallas was named after what person?
   GEORGE DALLAS
7. What football game is held in Dallas on New Year's Day?
   COTTON BOWL
8. Near what city is the Alamo located?
   SAN ANTONIO
9. What city is close to Palo Duro Canyon in the panhandle?
   AMARILLO
10. What city takes its name from the Spanish term for "the pass"?
    EL PASO
11. What popular resort city has Mustang Island in its bay?
    CORPUS CHRISTI
12. Where is "Tornado Alley"?
    The RED RIVER VALLEY
13. What kind of storm forms over the Gulf of Mexico, often hitting the Texas coast?
    HURRICANES
14. What is the richest natural resource in Texas?
    PETROLEUM (LAND MAY ALSO BE ACCEPTED)
15. Name three rivers that form boundaries for the state of Texas.
    RED RIVER   RIO GRANDE RIVER   SABINE RIVER
16. What are the two major uses of land in Texas?
    FARMING AND RANCHING
17. What is the name of a large wooded area in eastern Texas?
    PINEY WOODS
18. Texas produces more of which fishing product than any other state.
    SHRIMP

Name _____ **Standard: History**

American Settlers

During the late 1700's, the United States gained its independence from England. In 1803 the country bought the territory of Louisiana, bringing the United States boundaries up to the Texas line. People living near Texas became even more interested in this area. Between the years of 1820 and 1836 over 40,000 people from the United States came to Texas to settle. Texas was still under Spanish rule at the time.

Moses Austin was one of the first United States citizens to settle in Texas. He wanted to start a colony in this territory so he asked permission from the Spanish governor. In 1821 he was given permission to bring 300 United States families to Texas, but he died before he could carry out his plan. His son, Stephen, took over the effort.

During that same year (1821) Mexico became independent of Spain, and Texas was now under the Mexican flag. Stephen Austin, wanting to carry on with his father's work, made a new agreement with Mexico. He would be allowed to bring settlers to Texas, but they must become Mexican citizens and Roman Catholics. Austin returned to the United States and advertised for people wanting to move to Texas. He offered inexpensive land to law abiding citizens. Over the next ten years Austin brought about 6,000 United States citizens to Texas.

Austin was not the only one to receive permission for a colony in Texas. The idea of settling in an "untamed" land was exciting, and many people from the United States came to give it a try. Life in Texas was not easy for the new settlers. Men, women, and children had to work very hard and had little free time. The threat of Indian raids was always there. Droughts made it impossible for farmers to grow anything. At other times there was too much rain, or seeds were not available to plant. Even though life was difficult, few colonists gave up and returned to the United States. Most of them endured the hardships and made a living as best they could. By 1836 the population in Texas had grown to about 50,000.

1. Which country controlled Texas when Stephen Austin began the new colony?
   SPAIN

Give two reasons why life in Texas was difficult for new settlers:

2. **INDIAN RAIDS**
3. **DROUGHTS**

Mexico asked Stephen Austin to make settlers agree to do what two things?

4. **BECOME MEXICAN CITIZENS**
5. **BECOME ROMAN CATHOLIC**

Name _____ **Standard: History**

Who Am I?

Read each description on the right and decide who it describes.
Write the letter of the correct person or group on each line.

A. Caddo
B. Comanche
C. de Pineda
D. de Vaca
E. Jumanos
F. Karankawa
G. La Salle
H. Sam Houston
I. Santa Anna
J. Stephen Austin
K. Tigua
L. William Travis

F — An Indian tribe that lived along the coast and loved dogs.

E — West Texas Indians who grew corn and hunted buffalo.

A — This tribe called themselves "Tashas", or friends.

B — Indian nomads and horse riders who relied on the buffalo for their survival.

K — One of two Indian tribes remaining in Texas today.

C — The first known Spanish explorer to come to Texas.

D — He was taken prisoner and heard about seven golden cities in Texas.

G — The first French explorer to colonize Texas.

J — A colonizer who brought 300 families from the United States to settle in Texas.

I — A Mexican general who became president.

L — He led the Texans at the Alamo.

H — He led the Texan army that defeated Santa Anna at San Jacinto.

Name _____ **Standard: History**

Joining the Union

After the 1836 war against Mexico, Texas became an independent country named the Republic of Texas. Sam Houston became the first president of this country as it raised a new flag and issued its own money. Both the flag and the money were designed around one star, so the country quickly became known as the "Lone Star Republic". Life as an independent country had its problems as Texas struggled with disputes over establishing a border with Mexico, experienced Indian wars, and suffered financial problems. Many Texans, including Sam Houston, wanted to become a state of the United States. In September 1836, Texas voted to join the union. It was not quickly accepted by Congress, however, because Texas allowed slavery. Many of the early settlers had come from southern states and brought their slaves with them. Most of the northern states were against slavery and were not eager to have another state that allowed it. The debate in Congress continued for nine years, but Texas was admitted to the union as the 28th state on December 29, 1845.

The border disputes with Mexico had become a big problem. In 1846 (only a few months after Texas joined the union) the United States and Mexico went to war. The U.S. victory in 1848 established the Rio Grande as the border between the two counties. Texas claimed all the land along the Rio Grande as far as southern Colorado. Their new territory included what today is half of New Mexico and parts of Colorado, Wyoming, Oklahoma, and Kansas. The northern states were against expanding Texas because they did not want slavery to be allowed in the new territory. In the Compromise of 1850, Texas agreed to give up its claim to those lands in exchange for ten million dollars. By 1850, the population of Texas was 212,000. It tripled in the next ten years, rising to 600,000 by 1860.

1. What was the name of the independent country that Texas became in 1836?
   THE REPUBLIC OF TEXAS
2. Why was this country nicknamed the "Lone Star Republic"?
   IT HAD ONLY ONE STAR ON THE FLAG
3. Why wasn't Texas immediately accepted as a state when it applied in 1836?
   THE UNION DIDN'T WANT ANOTHER SLAVE SUPPORTING STATE

After the war with Mexico, Texas owned part of five other states. Name them.

4. **NEW MEXICO**
5. **COLORADO**
6. **WYOMING**
7. **OKLAHOMA**
8. **TEXAS**

ANSWER KEYS: 36, 39, 40, 41

Name _____ Standard: History

Find the Facts

1. In what month and year did Texas first vote to join the Union?
   SEPTEMBER 1836

2. Why did it take nine years for Texas to be admitted to the Union?
   TEXAS ALLOWED SLAVERY. THE UNION DID NOT WANT TO ADMIT ANOTHER SLAVE STATE.

3. What river became the border between Texas and Mexico in the year 1848?
   THE RIO GRANDE

4. On what date did Texas secede from the Union? **FEBRUARY 1, 1861**

5. Who was Jefferson Davis? **PRESIDENT OF THE CONFEDERATE STATES OF AMERICA (THE SOUTH)**

6. The most important Civil War battles fought in Texas were over which city? Why?
   GALVESTON BECAUSE IT WAS AN IMPORTANT PORT USED TO BRING SUPPLIES AND TRADE TO THE SOUTH

7. What was Reconstruction? **A PERIOD OF REBUILDING AFTER THE CIVIL WAR**

8. Which resource helped Texas recover from the economic loses after the war?
   CATTLE

The following statements refer to either the North or South during the Civil War. Write "N" on the blank if it is about the North and "S" if it is about the South.

- **N** It was called the Union.
- **N** Lincoln was the president.
- **S** They lost the war.
- **S** Won the battle at Palmito Hill.
- **N** Wanted to capture Galveston to cut off supplies imported there.
- **S** Jefferson Davis was the president.
- **N** Carpetbaggers were from here.
- **S** Eleven states that seceded because they wanted to keep slavery.

Name _____ Standard: History Graphics

Flags over Texas
There have been six flags flown over Texas during its history.
Find each flag and paste or draw a picture in the appropriate box below.

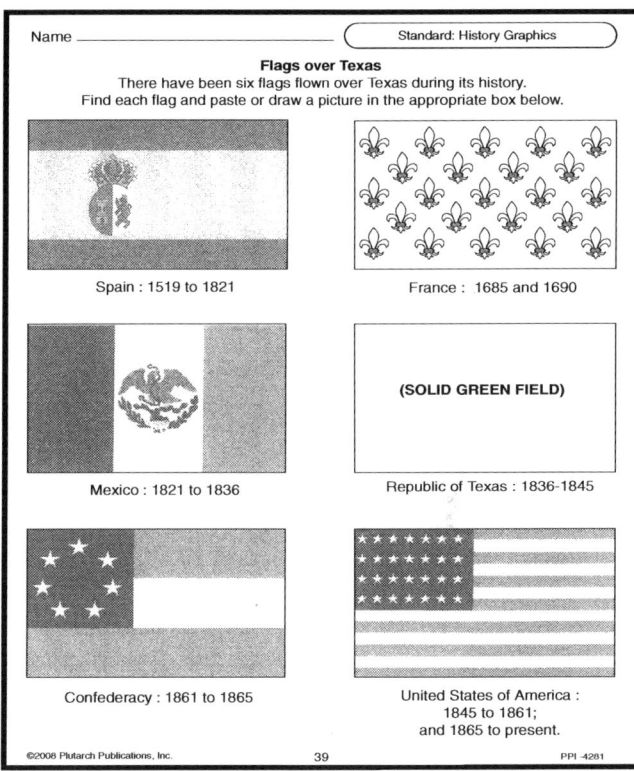

Spain: 1519 to 1821   France: 1685 and 1690

Mexico: 1821 to 1836   (SOLID GREEN FIELD) Republic of Texas: 1836-1845

Confederacy: 1861 to 1865   United States of America: 1845 to 1861; and 1865 to present.

Name _____ Standard: History Graphics

History Time line
Fill in the time line below by writing the correct name of each country on the line below the years its flag flew over Texas.

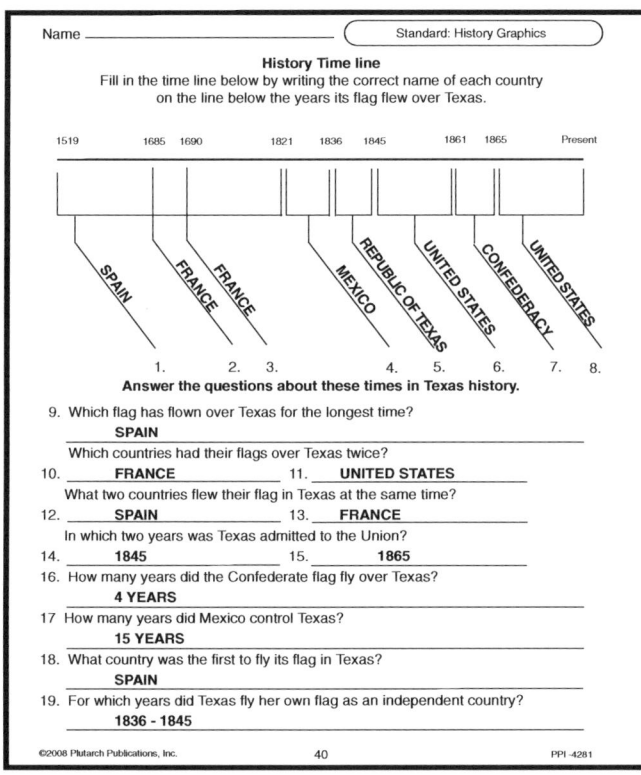

Answer the questions about these times in Texas history.

9. Which flag has flown over Texas for the longest time?
   SPAIN
   Which countries had their flags over Texas twice?
10. **FRANCE**   11. **UNITED STATES**
    What two countries flew their flag in Texas at the same time?
12. **SPAIN**   13. **FRANCE**
    In which two years was Texas admitted to the Union?
14. **1845**   15. **1865**
16. How many years did the Confederate flag fly over Texas?
    4 YEARS
17. How many years did Mexico control Texas?
    15 YEARS
18. What country was the first to fly its flag in Texas?
    SPAIN
19. For which years did Texas fly her own flag as an independent country?
    1836 - 1845

Name _____ Standard: History Graphics

Texas Time line
A time line helps show historical events in the order in which they happened. Below is a time line showing the sequence of events leading to Texas becoming a state.

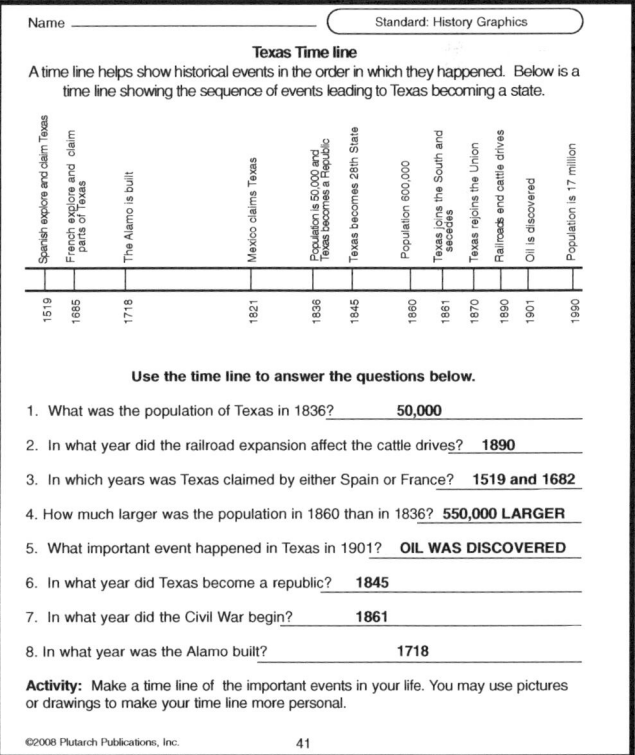

Use the time line to answer the questions below.

1. What was the population of Texas in 1836? **50,000**
2. In what year did the railroad expansion affect the cattle drives? **1890**
3. In which years was Texas claimed by either Spain or France? **1519 and 1682**
4. How much larger was the population in 1860 than in 1836? **550,000 LARGER**
5. What important event happened in Texas in 1901? **OIL WAS DISCOVERED**
6. In what year did Texas become a republic? **1845**
7. In what year did the Civil War begin? **1861**
8. In what year was the Alamo built? **1718**

Activity: Make a time line of the important events in your life. You may use pictures or drawings to make your time line more personal.

ANSWER KEYS: 42, 43, 45, 47

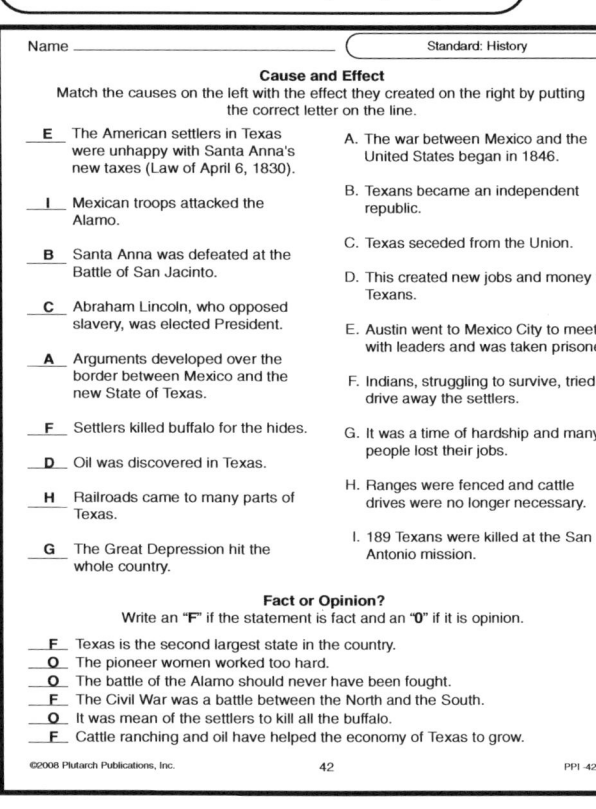

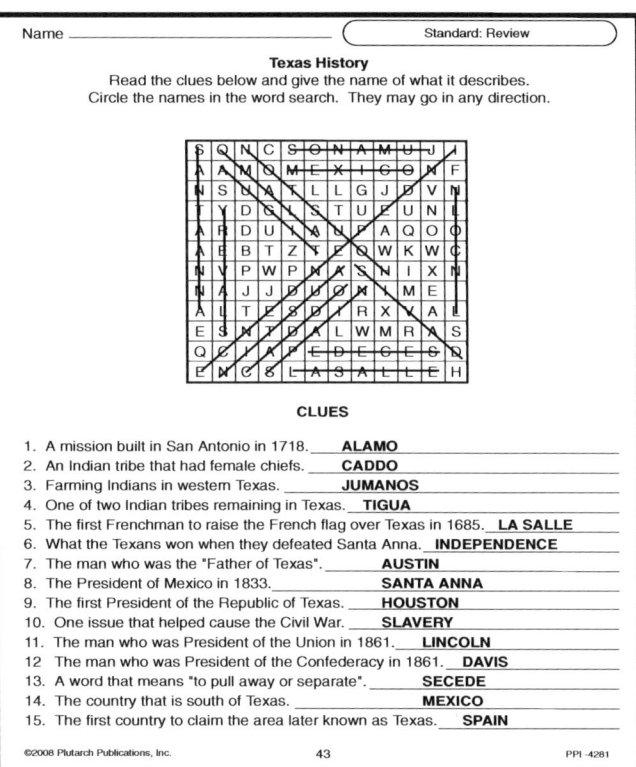

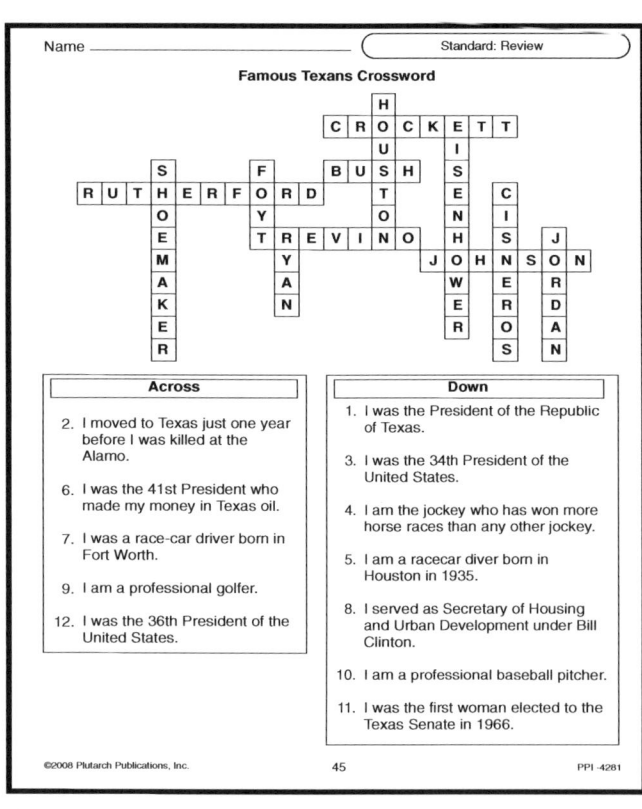

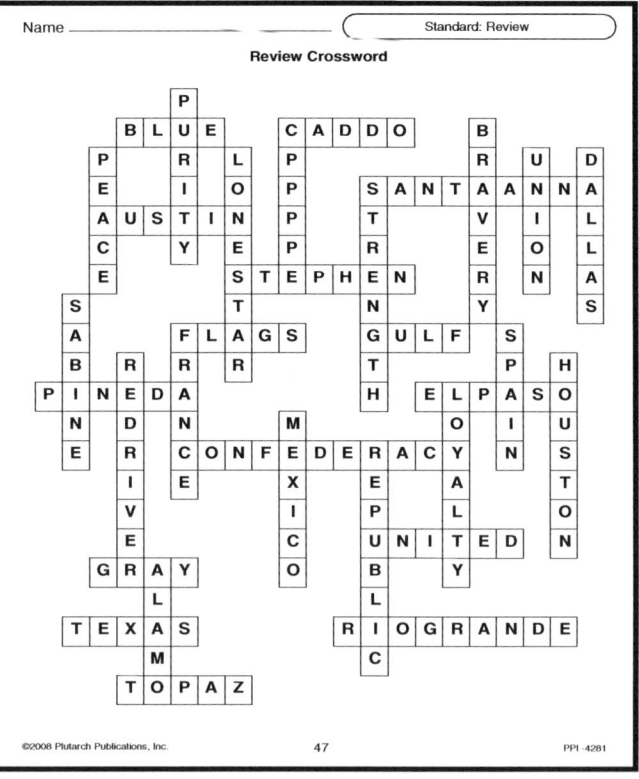

ANSWER KEYS: 48, 49, 50, 51

Fact or Opinion?
Write an "F" if the statement is fact and an "O" if it is opinion.

- **O** 1. Texas is the best state in which to live.
- **F** 2. Texas has a population of about 24 million.
- **O** 3. The Mexicans were wrong to attack the Alamo.
- **O** 4. Eastern Texas is the prettiest part of the state.
- **F** 5. Guadalupe Peak is the highest point in Texas.
- **F** 6. Eighty percent of the population lives in urban areas.
- **O** 7. The country is a nicer place to live than the city.
- **O** 8. The bluebonnet is the most beautiful flower that grows wild in Texas.
- **F** 9. The State Seal has olive and oak branches around the star.
- **F** 10. The mockingbird is white and gray.
- **O** 11. The mockingbird makes lovely mimicking noises.
- **F** 12. Pecan trees grow very well in Texas forests.
- **O** 13. Pecans are the most delicious nuts.
- **O** 14. Austin is the best place to hear live music.
- **F** 15. The Cotton Bowl is always played in Dallas.
- **F** 16. The Alamo is in San Antonio.
- **F** 17. El Paso is the Spanish Term for "the pass".
- **F** 18. Twenty-one percent of the Texas population is Hispanic.
- **O** 19. The mountains and basins region has the most spectacular sights in Texas.
- **O** 20. Oil is the best investment anyone can make.
- **F** 21. Cattle now graze where buffalo once did.
- **F** 22. Spain was the first country to raise its flag over Texas.
- **O** 23. Lyndon Johnson was a great President.
- **O** 24. Corpus Christi is the nicest resort area.
- **F** 25. The state gem is the topaz.
- **F** 26. The State Capital Building is made of pink granite.
- **F** 27. Austin is the capital of Texas.
- **O** 28. Texas raises the best cattle meat in the country.
- **F** 29. The Comanche and Apache tribes were nomads and great fighters.
- **O** 30. Using a time line is the best way to study Texas history.

Texas
Read the clues below and give the name of what it describes.
Circle the names in the word search. They may go in any direction.

CLUES

1. The state bird. — **MOCKINGBIRD**
2. The state gem. — **TOPAZ**
3. The olive branch on the State Seal symbolizes this. — **PEACE**
4. The oak branch on the State Seal symbolizes this. — **STRENGTH**
5. Home of the Cowboys football team. — **DALLAS**
6. The state tree. — **PECAN**
7. The state flower. — **BLUEBONNET**
8. What the color red symbolizes on the state flag. — **BRAVERY**
9. What the color white symbolizes on the state flag. — **PURITY**
10. The capital city. — **AUSTIN**
11. The 28th state to join the United States. — **TEXAS**
12. The city where helium is produced. — **AMARILLO**
13. A busy port city on the Gulf of Mexico. — **CORPUS CHRISTI**
14. The natural resource discovered in 1901. — **OIL**
15. Herds of these were once driven up the Chisholm Trail. — **CATTLE**
16. 80% of this resource is used for ranching and farming. — **LAND**
17. This group of fruits are grown in southern Texas. — **CITRUS**
18. A large city in western Texas. — **EL PASO**
19. 21% of the population is made of this ethnic group. — **HISPANIC**
20. This arena is located in Houston. — **ASTRODOME**

UNIT TEST

Part I
Read the statements and decide whether each is true or false.
On the blank, put 'T' if the statement is true and "O" if it is false.

- **T** 1. A star is at the center of the State Seal of Texas.
- **T** 2. Texas became a state in 1845.
- **O** 3. The state nickname is "Friendship".
- **O** 4. The Texas state flower is the daisy.
- **O** 5. The Spanish flag was the third one to be flown over Texas.
- **O** 6. Lyndon Johnson was not born in Texas, but he lived there most of his life.
- **T** 7. The Texas state capital building is made of pink granite.
- **O** 8. The Alamo was built near Houston.
- **T** 9. Santa Anna was a Mexican general and president.
- **T** 10. Texas is the second largest state in the country.

Part II
Write the correct answer for each blank.

11. The capital of Texas is — **AUSTIN**
12. The nickname for Texas is — **LONE STAR STATE**
13. The state bird is — **MOCKINGBIRD**
14. The olive branch on the State Seal of Texas stands for — **PEACE**
15. The color blue on the state flag stands for — **LOYALTY**

The four states that touch the Texas border are:
16. **LOUISIANA**
17. **ARKANSAS**
18. **OLKAHOMA**
19. **NEW MEXICO**
20. The body of water located southeast of Texas is — **GULF OF MEXICO**
21. The river that separates Texas and Mexico is the — **RIO GRANDE**

The four regions of Texas are:
22. **COASTAL PLAINS**
23. **NORTH CENTRAL PLAINS**
24. **GREAT PLAINS**
25. **MOUNTAINS AND BASINS**

Part III
Match each flag with the dates it flew over Texas.

- **A** 26. The Confederate flag — A. 1861-1865
- **B** 27. The French flag — B. 1685 and 1690
- **E** 28. The Mexican flag — C. 1836-1845
- **C** 29. The Republic of Texas flag — D. 1845-1861; 1865 to present
- **F** 30. The Spanish flag — E. 1821-1836
- **D** 31. The United States flag — F. 1519-1821

Part IV
Short answer

32. Name the state tree. — **PECAN**

Name the two leading economic resources of Texas:
33. A. **OIL, FISHING, TOURISM, MANUFACTURING (ANSWERS WILL VARY)**
34. B. **LAND, BANKING, INSURANCE, MINING**
35. What does the live oak branch on the State Seal stand for? — **PEACE**
36. What river lies between Texas and Louisiana? — **SABINE**
37. In which city would you find the Astrodome? — **HOUSTON**
38. Which city is known as the "Live Music Capital of the World"? — **AUSTIN**
39. Which city is also known as "The Alamo City"? — **SAN ANTONIO**
40. Where is the Cotton Bowl held every year? — **DALLAS**
41. The name of the area excellent for growing citrus fruits? — **THE VALLEY**
42. Which city is the world's largest producer of helium? — **AMARILLO**
43. Where is "Tornado Alley" located? — **RED RIVER VALLEY**
44. Which city lies across the Rio Grande from Juarez, Mexico? — **EL PASO**
45. The name of which city comes from the Spanish word for yellow? — **AMARILLO**
46. Name the region of Texas where the "Piney Woods" is found: — **EASTERN TEXAS**
47. Which region in west Texas has most of the mountains? — **MOUNTAINS & BASINS**
48. Which port city was important to Texas during the Civil War? — **GALVESTON**
49. Palo Duro canyon is just outside which city? — **AMARILLO**
50. What animal was brought in after the buffalo were gone? — **CATTLE**

©Plutarch Publications, Inc. PPI -4281

ANSWER KEYS: 52 - 53

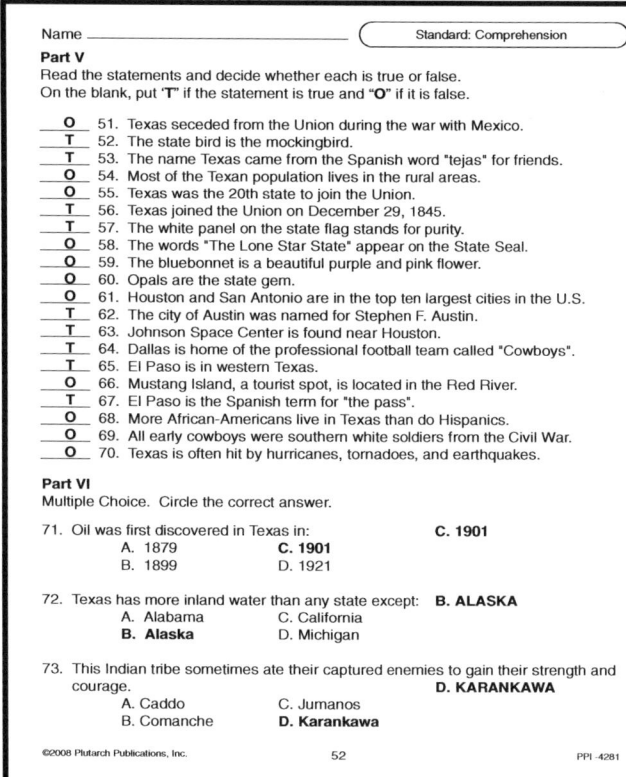

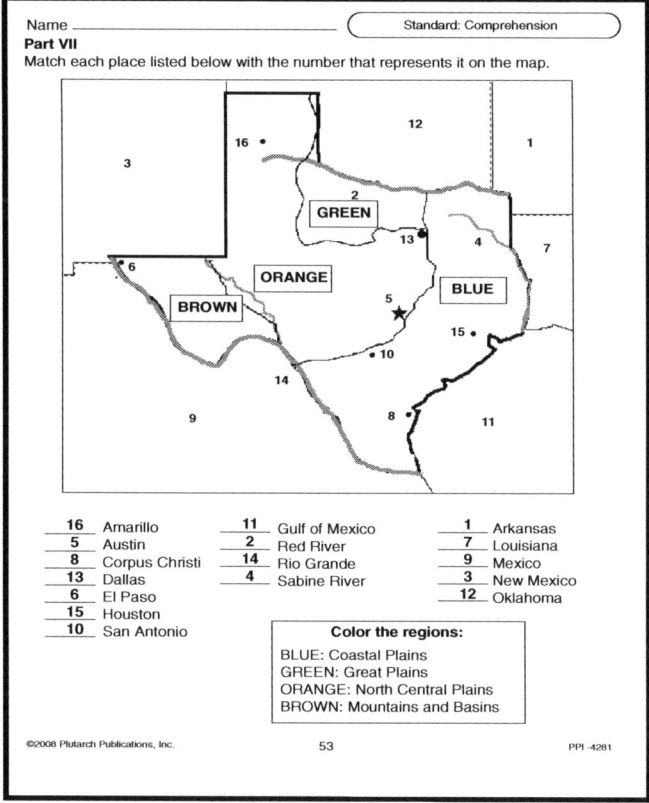

Made in the USA
Middletown, DE
22 February 2015